The Teacher's Guide to Successful Professional Learning Networks

The Teacher's Guide to Successful Professional Learning Networks

A practical guide to overcoming the challenges, negotiating the pitfalls and improving student outcomes

Cindy Poortman and Chris Brown

Open University Press

Open University Press
McGraw Hill
Unit 4
Foundation Park
Roxborough Way
Maidenhead
SL6 3UD

email: emea_uk_ireland@mheducation.com
world wide web: www.mheducation.co.uk

Copyright © Open International Publishing Limited, 2023

All rights reserved. Except for the quotation of short passages for the purposes of criticism and review, no part of this publication may be reproduced, stored in a retrieval system, or transmitted, in any form or by any means, electronic, mechanical, photocopying, recording or otherwise, without the prior written permission of the publisher or a licence from the Copyright Licensing Agency Limited. Details of such licences (for reprographic reproduction) may be obtained from the Copyright Licensing Agency Ltd of Saffron House, 6–10 Kirby Street, London EC1N 8TS.

Executive Editor: Eleanor Christie
Editorial Assistant: Phoebe Hills
Content Product Manager: Ali Davis

A catalogue record of this book is available from the British Library

ISBN-13: 9780335251087
ISBN-10: 0335251080
eISBN: 9780335251094

Library of Congress Cataloging-in-Publication Data
CIP data applied for

Typeset by Transforma Pvt. Ltd., Chennai, India

Fictitious names of companies, products, people, characters and/or data that may be used herein (in case studies or in examples) are not intended to represent any real individual, company, product or event.

Praise Page

"Now more than ever, teachers need to access the support, knowledge and share expertise and experiences of their peers. In this book, Cindy and Chris offer a framework that supports teachers to do just this. The establishment of professional learning networks can be transformational for you personally and professionally. This book takes you step by step through the process of developing an effective PLN to create and realise a new status quo!"
                    Catherine Carden, Canterbury Christ Church University, UK

"The publication impressively underscores the relevance and opportunities of Professional Learning Networks for innovation in schools. It also addresses the challenges and pitfalls of successfully establishing, running, and sustaining PLNs from the perspective of teachers. The text is a welcome invitation to understand education in schools and school development as a joint effort of professionals and to pool expertise."
                    Colin Cramer, University of Tuebingen, Germany

"This book is a must read for practitioners, policy makers and researchers interested in Professional Learning (PLN) Networks! The authors take the readers on an engaging, thoughtful, and inspiring journey focused on how to ensure not only the effectiveness but also the sustainability of (the work of) PLNs. The book provides the readers with concrete recipes with all the necessary ingredients, including leadership, trust, and collaboration, to ensure PLN success."
                    Prof. Dr. Kim Schildkamp, University of Twente, the Netherlands

Contents

A brief introduction vi

1 THE CALL TO ADVENTURE – REALIZING THE NEED FOR CHANGE 1
2 FINDING ALLIES WHEN FORMING A PROFESSIONAL LEARNING NETWORK 16
3 CHALLENGES AND PITFALLS – SUCCESSFULLY RUNNING AND SUSTAINING YOUR PLN 33
4 TRIALS AND REWARDS – ADOPTING CYCLES OF INQUIRY 48
5 THE RETURN – MOBILIZING FINDINGS AND GETTING BUY-IN 63
6 ACHIEVING A NEW STATUS QUO – MAKING NETWORKS AN EVERYDAY FEATURE OF SCHOOL LIFE 79

Index 89

A brief introduction

Many teachers and school leaders enjoy working together (within and across schools) to improve outcomes for students. Sharing their ways of working, ongoing challenges and new ideas helps them think out-of-the box and develop their teaching to better address students' needs. That's why, internationally, the focus on learning in networks has never been greater. At the same time, educators are regularly encountering practical problems related to, for example, time, resources and communication, as well as more fundamental issues in attempting to ensure their Professional Learning Networks (PLN) work effectively. How teachers can participate in networks to achieve deep reflective inquiry, to really make positive changes in teaching and learning, is not self-evident. As such, this book aims to help educators by providing practical guidelines developed from the authors' hands-on and research-based experience in this area. Taking a step-by-step approach, the book will take you through the different phases (establishing, process and scale-up), the stages of inquiry and the influencing factors (e.g. collaboration and leadership) that are involved in successfully running a PLN, drawing on a diverse range of real-life examples from projects situated across a range of international contexts.

What are PLNs?

We define a PLN as a group of educators coming together with others outside of their everyday community of practice, with the intention of engaging in collaborative learning to improve outcomes for students (Poortman et al., 2022: 13). Participants can be both school leaders and teachers, and they might also be working together with researchers and/or policymakers; but the recent emergence of PLNs worldwide is generally attributed to the need for teachers and other educators to continually learn and share this learning in order to provide an education that suits the requirements of the twenty-first century. Networks can focus on a vast range of outcomes – from issues of student well-being and equity to achievement outcomes. But PLNs are also a recognition that small numbers of teachers learning in networks can, if effective, lead to bottom-up system-level change (Brown, 2020).

Evidence suggests that PLNs can positively impact on:

- **the professional learning of teachers** participating within the PLN;
- **the innovation potential of participating schools** – in other words, the culture and capacity required to effectively create and spread new knowledge and practice within schools that have connections to networks;
- the **practice of teachers** – and as a result, improved **student outcomes**.

PLNs also provide the opportunity to **achieve cost-effective educational change at scale:** this is because they only require small numbers of teachers to leave their communities of practice to innovate (Katz and Earl, 2010; Berkemeyer et al., 2011; Armstrong, 2015; Brown, 2020).

But the benefits outlined above are not guaranteed, and it is important that this is recognized by those potentially turning to PLNs as a means to improve teaching and learning. Furthermore, the impact of engaging in a PLN should not be considered sustainable until it results in lasting school-wide changes in school policy and practice, with these changes resulting in measurably positive outcomes (Brown, 2020). So how can we go about establishing a successful PLN that lasts the course? Rather than a set of hoops to jump through, we like to see the journey towards networked learning as a form of adventure. Like any good adventure, this journey is filled with challenges to be overcome and pitfalls to be negotiated before our goals can be reached. In *The Hero with a Thousand Faces* (1949), Joseph Campbell suggests that the basis for most of the heroic quests that feature in the myths and legends of any society can be distilled down to a six-step cycle. Seeing the similarity with the journey towards fostering effective PLNs, we have adopted a slightly modified version of Campbell's cycle, resulting in six key steps for establishing and running effective PLNs:

1. The call to adventure – realizing the need for change;
2. Finding allies – forming a Professional Learning Network;
3. Challenges and pitfalls – successfully running and sustaining your PLN;
4. Trials and rewards – adopting cycles of inquiry;
5. The return – mobilizing findings and getting buy-in; and
6. Achieving a new status quo – making networks an everyday feature of school life.

This cycle is illustrated in Figure 0.1.

Figure 0.1: Six key steps for establishing and running effective PLNs

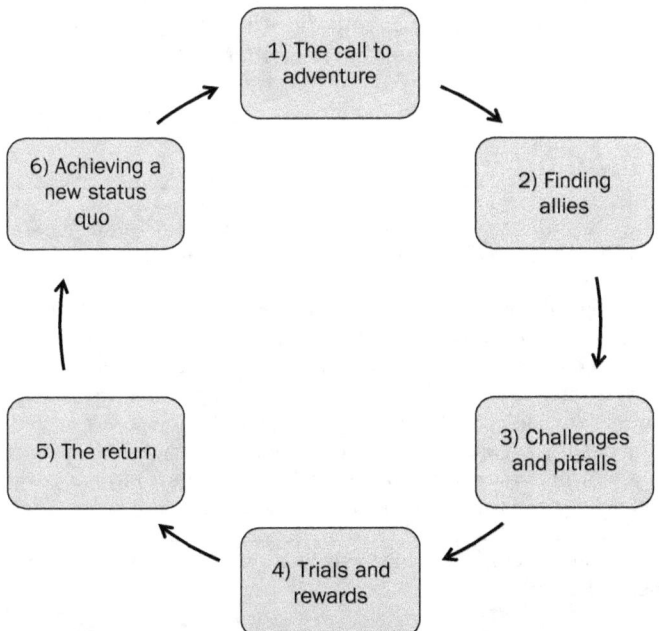

Consequently, we have used these six steps to structure the book. As a result, each chapter provides a comprehensive step-by-step guide for each of the six steps in Figure 0.1 above, drawing on case studies or using illustrative vignettes to spotlight effective and ineffective practices. Each chapter also includes summaries to indicate:

1. your role [i.e. the role of the educator currently reading this];
2. what will be needed from formal (responsible!) school leaders; and
3. the role of others in your PLN and your school.

Furthermore, we also conclude, in Chapter 6, with a PLN health check (a combined PLN compass and map, if you will) for you to use to make sure you are on the right track.

So, in a nutshell, with this book we have provided you with everything you will need for your heroic quest, and to be able to successfully navigate the path in front of you. We sincerely hope you enjoy engaging with the text and our ideas ... and we wish you good luck on the adventure ahead!

Cindy and Chris, September 2022

Acknowledgement

The insights on which this book are based were developed through our work with educators and co-researchers in research, workshops, (guest) lectures, conferences, and through reviewing extant research in this area of the past decades. We would like to thank all of those who contributed by participating in this work, and especially the members of the ICSEI network *Professional Learning Networks*,[1] for their valuable contribution to the field.

Further reading

Armstrong, P. (2015) *Effective Partnerships and Collaboration for School Improvement: A Review of the Evidence*. London: Department for Education.

Berkemeyer, N., Järvinen, H. and Bos, W. (2011) Unterricht gemeinsam entwickeln. Eine Bilanz nach vier Jahren schulischer Netzwerkarbeit, *Pädagogik*, 11(11): 46–51.

Brown, C. (2020) *The Networked School Leader: How to Improve Teaching and Student Outcomes Using Learning Networks*. London: Emerald.

Brown, C. and Poortman, C. (2020) Professional Learning Networks: Promises and challenges for sustainable school improvement. Contribution to a newsletter from the Valu.E project (https://value.invalsi.it/portale/en/home-english/). Available at https://value.invalsi.it/portale/en/magazine/professional-learning-networks-promises-and-challenges-for-sustainable-school-improvement-2/

---

1 International Congress for School Effectiveness and Improvement: https://www.icsei.net/professional-learning/

Campbell, J. (2008 [1949]) *The Hero with a Thousand Faces*, Bollingen Series Vol. 17. Novato, CA: New World Library (originally published by Pantheon Books).

Katz, S. and Earl, L. (2010) Learning about networked learning communities, *School Effectiveness and School Improvement*, 21(1): 27–51.

Poortman, C.L., Brown, C. and Schildkamp, K. (2022) Professional Learning Networks: A conceptual model and research opportunities, *Educational Research*, 64(1): 95–112. https://doi.org/10.1080/00131881.2021.1985398

1 The call to adventure – realizing the need for change

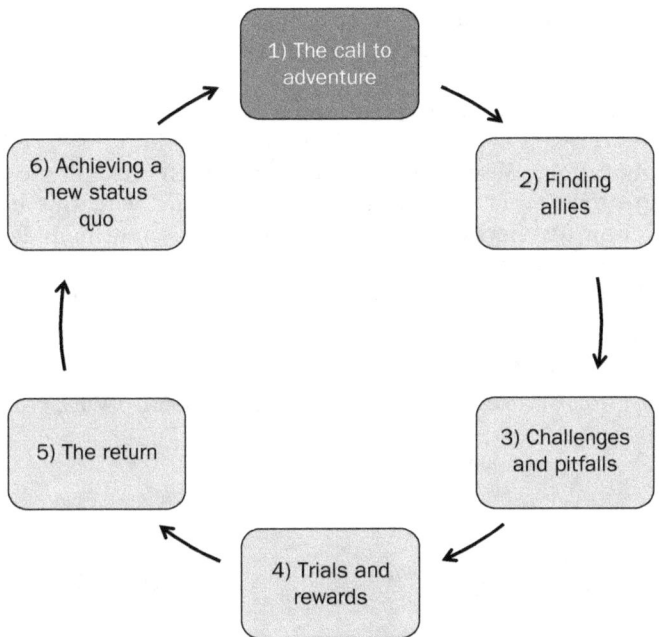

The PLN adventure starts with a problem that teachers (teachers, school leaders, teaching assistants and others) find themselves unable to tackle alone. Schools are faced with many challenges in their daily practice, e.g. concerning students' social-emotional well-being, students' language achievement, or questions such as how teachers can develop effective lesson series for improving students' science knowledge and skills. Very often, teachers up and down the country – maybe even globally – face similar problems, despite differences in their regions and schools. The (post-)Covid era also comes with even more salient challenges, such as those regarding equality and digital education. Addressing these problems would not only benefit teachers and their colleagues, but – most importantly of all – it would also benefit their students, as well as teachers and students in other schools.

Teachers facing these kinds of problems know, deep down, that resolving them requires meaningful collaboration if they are to be addressed effectively. But effective collaboration both within and across schools can often be rarer than a blue moon. For instance, analysis undertaken by Fraser and Fulop (2022), of the 2018 Teaching and Learning International Survey (TALIS), suggests that collaboration can be thought of as comprising either: i) exchange and coordination for teaching, which consists of looser forms of informal collaboration; or ii) professional collaboration, which involves frequent, deep and regular forms of collaboration amongst teachers, and presents vital opportunities for teachers to collaborate directly to improve instructional processes in the classroom. Yet of these two, as we show in Figure 1.1, this professional collaboration activity is far less prevalent than simple exchanges and coordination between teachers. And this is true across the globe.

So, given this gap between ideal and real, what are the steps teachers need to take to reach beyond their classroom door in order to begin meaningful collaboration? We will cover this topic in both this and the next chapter, looking at different aspects in turn. We begin, with this chapter, by considering how teachers can galvanize collaboration through developing a shared sense of purpose focused on outcomes for students, as well as illustrating the kind of thorny issues where Professional Learning Networks can provide most help.

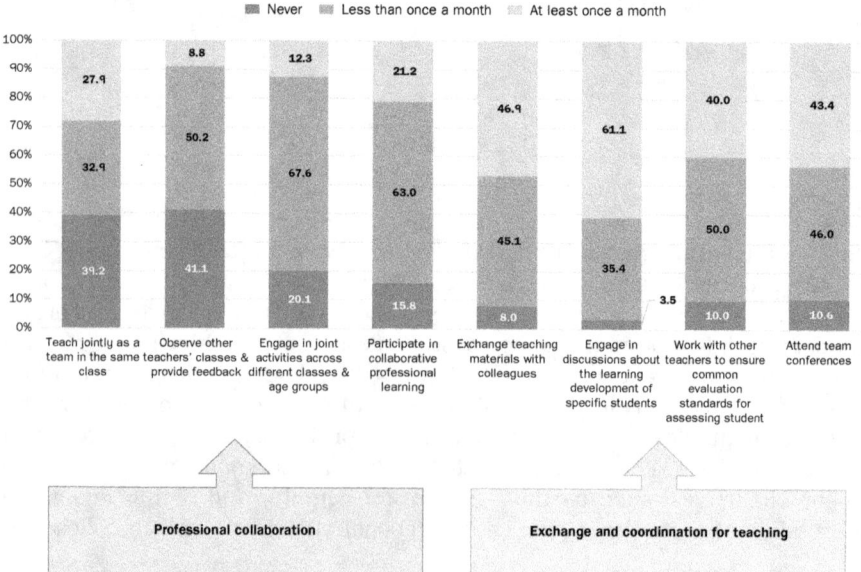

Figure 1.1 Frequency of professional collaboration activity compared with exchange and coordination

So, what's your goal? And is it just your goal?

Engaging in the kind of reflective practice needed to address challenges in student outcomes requires PLN participants to agree on a goal focused on a concrete outcome. Specifically, PLN members need to develop a shared sense of purpose focused on student learning (Poortman and Brown, 2018) – in other words, to 'own the problem'. We say 'develop' because, coming from different schools and specific contexts, this is not likely to be the case straight from the get-go. Individual educators and their schools may have varying reasons for participating in PLNs. Some schools may have a more general goal of teacher professional development in mind, for instance, but their teachers may be experiencing a specific problem in their daily practice that they want to address. What's more, colleagues, both within the same school as well as from other schools, might think differently about what the nature of their problem is. But it's not an issue if goals at the PLN level, the school/cross-school level and individual levels are not identical right away. At the same time, the PLN will not be effective if such goals contradict each other. PLN participants thus need to use the initial (or start-up) phase of PLN activity to discuss and exchange ideas about their focus, keeping in mind that the aim of developing this shared sense of purpose should be centred on and grounded in student learning. This provides vision and direction for later activity, and will have a significant impact on teaching practice (Earl and Katz, 2006).

Main starting points for the need for change

When we consider the drivers for change that lead to educators engaging in a PLN, we can see that they are usually driven either from the top down or from the bottom up. Starting with the former, it is clear that the direction of educational policy in many Western countries has changed dramatically in recent years. As a result there has been a rapid shift away from the government-managed educational changes of the 1990s and 2000s, to far more decentralized systems based on the principle of school 'autonomy' and school 'self-improvement' (Hopkins, 2022). Consequently, many central government policy initiatives now involve a networked approach to implementation. In other words, they present a top-down impetus for change which needs to be delivered via a PLN. For instance, recent curriculum reform in the Australian federal state of New South Wales utilizes Teacher Engagement Networks (TENs) to support the roll-out of the new curriculum. The aims of the TENs are to: i) provide feedback, input and advice to inform the development of curriculum support materials and professional development priorities; and ii) support implementation of curriculum reforms in the schools and regions. By way of another top-down example, Ontario's Teacher Learning and Leadership Program (TLLP) represented an approach to teacher development that centred on teachers leading their own professional learning (Campbell et al., 2016). The TLLP began in 2007 as a joint initiative between the Ontario Ministry of Education and the Ontario Teachers' Federation, with aims to:

1. Create and support opportunities for teacher professional learning;
2. Foster teacher leadership; and
3. Facilitate the sharing of exemplary practices for the broader benefit of Ontario's students.

(Ontario Ministry of Education, n.d.: 3)

For their TLLP proposals, teachers self-identified an area of practice or an issue that they were interested in investigating, which also had the potential to benefit other students and/or schools more widely (Campbell et al., 2016: 227). At the end of their TLLP projects, TLLP teams attended the Sharing the Learning Summit, which enabled them to showcase completed projects and to share their practices. In addition, to further spread learning from their projects, school districts could also apply for Provincial Knowledge Exchange funding to provide resources for release time and travel to enable TLLP teacher leaders to share their knowledge and practices with other teachers, schools and school districts across Ontario (Campbell et al., 2016: 223).

Recent bottom-up examples where educators have sought to tackle pressing educational problems include:

1. **Virtual PLNs in Calgary** to alleviate the effects of disruption from Covid-19 on students with learning difficulties. This was seen as vital since such students experienced disproportionately adverse effects from the loss of structure and stability caused by the pandemic, which many relied on for both their learning and mental health (Braunberger and Hamilton, 2022).
2. **Research Learning Networks for Looked After Children** – designed to support subject leads and designated teachers across England. The network focuses on specific areas related to maths and English that are beneficial to improving primary outcomes for this vulnerable group.
3. The work of the **Education Development Trust**, an educational charity, which works with some 2000 schools in England to strengthen collaborative school improvement through the practice of peer review (Cameron and Farrar, 2022) – a process that enables participating schools to systematically review and address weaknesses and share effective practice with one another.
4. Regional networks developed by the **Church of England Foundation for Educational Leadership** to support senior leaders in small rural schools in England (Greany and Wolfe, 2022).

Interwoven, and somewhat implicit, amongst all of these examples is a sense of moral imperative, with educators ultimately motivated by a commitment to social justice and doing the best they can for each child (Strike, 2007). As Day and Sammons (2013) note, if teachers and school leaders are to be considered successful, they should be promoting both academic and social outcomes for all students: with social outcomes including integrity, compassion and fairness, students possessing a love of lifelong learning, and schools fostering citizenship as well as personal, economic and social capabilities. Begley and Johansson (2003) go one step further, arguing that highly effective leaders are de facto characterized by their strong moral and ethical purposes and a strong sense of social justice. An underpinning assumption for the work presented in this book, therefore, is that both teachers and school leaders have, as their driving purpose, a desire to support all children and young people to be the best they can be – with the notion of 'being the best' considered to have a wide and socially just basis. It is achieving this purpose via a PLN approach that we believe will help educators secure the maximum impact possible.

PLN initiatives may also have a combination of top-down and bottom-up dimensions. In a four-year PLN project, for example, the **Dutch Ministry of Education** provided funding for teachers to participate in networks focused on a teaching subject (e.g. geography, English language), doing research in their schools, or a combination of the two (e.g. the Lesson Study approach). A total of 23 networks were established, guided by external coaches for a maximum of four years, while academics studied educators' resulting satisfaction, learning and application to practice. PLN coaching and the related research was funded by the Ministry; however, schools signed up on a voluntary basis and the PLNs could freely determine their goals and subjects (Prenger et al., 2019). Likewise, in the Dutch **datateam®** procedure (e.g. Schildkamp et al., 2016), schools could also voluntarily sign up for projects funded by the Ministry or large Dutch school boards. Coaching and research was (co-)funded, but the data teams were free to formulate their own specific problem and determine the goal they wanted to work on. Even though working on their own goals is often key for the intrinsic motivation of the participants (and their schools), the policy context and school (board) context are important factors for the PLN process, which is why a combination of top-down and bottom-up initiatives can often be ideal if PLNs are to thrive.

Criteria for defining your shared focus on student learning

Once we have a common topic or area for investigation, we can then focus down on the specific change or set of changes we want to see for, or in, our students. As noted above, these changes do not need to be uniform across the PLN, but they do need to be agreed on among those participating from the same school. A good way to illustrate what we mean here is by looking at the example of **Research Learning Networks (RLNs)**. RLNs (an example we will come back to throughout the book) involve small groups of teachers coming together from a number of schools to focus on tackling key issues related to teaching and learning. Although a form of PLN, RLNs are distinct in that there is an explicit focus on educators learning from and building on existing academic knowledge. The RLN model involves participants attending four workshops over the course of an academic year (October to June), with the content of these workshops as follows:

- **Workshop one:** participants focus on understanding the research and current practitioner held knowledge about the specific issues being explored (for example, how to ensure children develop growth mindsets). In this workshop they also gain an understanding of what impact might look like, and how (and what) to collect in order to establish the baseline (i.e. the here and now) picture.
- **Workshop two:** participants explore the baseline in more detail, develop a research-informed approach to improving practice within each school and consider how this approach might be trailed effectively.
- **Workshop three:** participants are enabled to refine their approaches; this workshop is also used to introduce the idea of whole-school change as well as change tools and change approaches.
- **Workshop four:** participants consider both the impact their work has achieved and how to share knowledge of impact more widely.

What is clear from this description of the RLN approach, and in particular workshops one and four, is that there needs to be an understanding of what change in student outcomes (and so teaching practice) is required, as well as an awareness of whether this change has been realized. To do this, RLN facilitators take workshop participants through a suite of exercises. The first, premised on the idea that great professional development starts with 'the end in mind' (Stoll et al., 2012), asks participants to imagine what the future holds in 12 months' time. Given the problem or focus area in question (for instance, how to develop more inclusive practices for looked after students), RLN participants are asked to consider 'what difference do you want to make?' and 'what will success look like?' Specifically, participants are encouraged to think deeply about, in relation to their given teaching and learning focus area: i) what students will be 'achieving' and 'doing'; ii) how students will be 'feeling'; iii) what will students be 'saying'; and iv) how will students be 'responding', if the new approaches that participants hope to develop prove to be effective. To support this exercise, proformas such as that set out in Figure 1.2, as well as related data capture mats, are utilized.

Having considered the difference they want to make, participants then repeat the exercise in terms of the actions and behaviours they might engage in that would lead to this change in students. Getting participants to think about future success in this way means that they can come to a common understanding of, and a vision for, what needs to be achieved – and this helps ensure the views of school participants are in alignment, so providing a foundation for action. Of course, a concrete understanding of the current situation is required before any action commences (otherwise, how else might we understand if impact has occurred?). So let's now look at how to arrive at a comprehensive picture of the here and now.

The call to adventure 7

Figure 1.2 Proforma for discussion

In school groups discuss: *What difference do you want to make? What will success look like?* (10 min)

Building our understanding of the problem

Having identified a problem area, we next need to drill down deeply into what is currently known about it, as well as into the types of approaches that might help us reach our desired vision for student outcomes. To begin with, PLN participants need a way of measuring the 'baseline' so that we know *exactly* what the gap between the vision and current situation is and, over time, whether we are closing it. Baseline data also helps us to firm up our understanding in relation to potential causes of this gap and so what interventions we might want to put in place to change the current situation. Questions to ask when thinking about collecting baseline data include:

1. What data needs to be collected?
2. What does this data concern ... students? Your practice? Your team?
3. Is this data readily available or do you need to collect it?
4. If you need additional data, what methods will you use and why?

While the nature of the baseline you collect will be specific to your context and focus area, we provide some examples of the types of data you might want to consider in Box 1.1. Looking at these examples, what can you use that will provide a meaningful measurement in terms of your current situation and, over time, whether you are heading towards your vision? What might be missing from this list? Vitally, how might you collect the data you need?

> **Box 1.1 Suggestions for collecting baseline data**
>
> **Evidence checklist**
>
> **Quantitative data**
>
> - attendance
> - attainment/teacher assessment
> - numbers attending at meetings or other sessions (parents/staff/children)
> - student and parent satisfaction survey data
> - student information systems and learning management systems data as well as other Big Data sources*
>
> **Qualitative data**
>
> Teacher–student role:
>
> - teacher assessments (statements) of target students
> - student self-evaluation/feedback
> - work samples (writing/drawing)
> - photographs
> - marking
> - reports from staff
> - individual behaviour plans
> - student voice
>
> Parent–child:
>
> - feedback from parents/carers
> - home–school communications
>
> **Research methodology**
>
> - questionnaire and analysis
> - interview questions and transcript
> - reflective diary/journal
> - lesson study/student observations
> - student/classroom discussion and transcript
> - student writing and analysis (e.g. diagnostic writing tools)
> - recorded data – audio/visual and analysis
> - data analytics of student or other forms of Big Data
>
> ---
>
> * Please note that while data use is a field on its own and going into related approaches and issues in-depth is beyond the scope of this book, we do want to emphasize the importance of data ethics.

As well as the baseline, there are two other vital sources of information that can help us firm up our understanding of the problem and the common foci we might all support: i) educators' own knowledge (as well as that of other PLN participants); and ii) current research knowledge (i.e. that produced by universities or other research-producing organizations). With Research Learning Networks, workshop protocols and exercises are used to enable RLN participants to bring together 'what is known' (i.e. existing research knowledge) with what they know about their context, their students and what they currently see as effective practice (i.e. their experience and the experience of others) (Brown, 2018). Overall, we refer to this process as 'knowledge creation' (Nonaka and Takeuchi, 1995; Brown and Rogers, 2015; see Box 1.2).

> **Box 1.2 Knowledge creation**
>
> **Knowledge creation** is a way of bringing together what educators know – their practical and contextual knowledge – with what research suggests might be effective. Knowledge creation thus enables teachers to combine these two sets of knowledge to create contextually appropriate teaching strategies that build on established approaches, but are also likely to be successful in their school or classroom.

Let's look at an example, which helps make explicit 'what educators know'. Here RLN participants use a data capture mat to help them consider, discuss and record:

1 an aspect of their practice that 'works' in relation to the topic area;
2 the absolute best practice in their school in relation to the topic area; and
3 the basis for making these statements, i.e. what's the evidence for their claims?

After exploring and providing challenges in relation to the responses to each of these questions (especially the evidence for making these claims), each RLN participant is then presented with an overarching 'literature review' that sets out 'what is known' in relation to the focus area for the RLN. The purpose of these reviews is to present research-informed principles and recommendations that can be employed as part of finding or developing solutions to the problem in hand. In order to build capacity and to ensure that subsequent learning conversations are genuinely challenging (we cover what we mean by learning conversations in more detail in Chapter 3), the content of these reviews is designed to move participants out of their comfort zones and to question their current practice.

Engaging with research literature

If you want to have a go at creating these types of reviews yourself, we have found that a useful starting point can be existing research syntheses, meta-analyses and comprehensive literature reviews. For instance, Hattie's (2013) 'Visible Learning' is a synthesis of over 800 meta-analyses, involving some 50,000 studies, or you could look at publicly available evidence such as that provided by the Education Endowment Foundation's 'toolkit', and the UCL IOE's Evidence for Policy and Practice Information and Co-ordinating (EPPI) Centre. Having found a selection of high-quality studies, these can then be brought together to provide a comprehensive overarching depiction of the subject in question. To maximize their usefulness, we have also found that it helps to set out the literature under the following headings:

1. **Method**: in order to help with educator capacity building, this section should provide detail on the sources used – *who* produced it, *why* they did so, *what* they did and *how*? Also, key detail on the sample involved, and so on.
2. **Overview of the issue or subject** in question and some of the key issues, debates or key drivers in relation to the issue/subject. In other words, as well as providing detail on the nature of the subject in hand, this section should specify what might be causing it, and/or the key components practitioners need to have in mind when considering it.
3. **Options for addressing some of these key issues and debates:** if present, practical 'solutions' to think about in relation to point 2 above, and/or challenging questions that the review raises in relation to existing practice, can also be presented.
4. **Potential issues to consider re implementation:** these might include, for instance, financial cost, time, staff understanding and capacity.

In order to introduce RLN participants to the research evidence relating to their focus area, it is also helpful to draw on exercises developed by Stoll and Brown (2015) as part of their knowledge transfer project (*Middle Leaders as Catalysts for Evidence-Informed Change*). Here, rather than ask practitioners to engage directly with the literature reviews, user-friendly strategies are used so that the key messages from research literature can be readily understood and imbibed. This is in keeping with the need to ensure that: i) 'formal' research knowledge is blended with individuals' surfaced tacit knowledge; ii) research knowledge is encountered in manageable units of meaning and in accessible formats; and iii) research knowledge is engaged with as part of a social process of meaning making (Stoll and Brown, 2015).

One example of such a strategy is known as the 'strips exercise'. Here research literature is introduced as strips or nuggets of information – i.e. the main content of each literature review developed is turned into small 'bite size' chunks, with these then printed and cut into strips of paper. Participants are then asked to work in pairs or threes to discuss each strip or nugget and allocate it a meaning (a theme), and to then iteratively develop these themes as they work their way through the strips.

Application to practitioners' knowledge and practice

Following this, participants are asked to complete a 'data capture' mat, a proforma (an example of which is provided below) which asks participants to consider how the research and the resultant themes:

1 connect with their own knowledge and practice (as expressed in the first exercise);
2 deepen their own knowledge and practice (as expressed in the first exercise); and
3 challenge their own knowledge and practice (as expressed in the first exercise) (see Box 1.3).

Participants are then provided with overall and individual literature reviews for their topic areas. The next thing participants must do, of course, is to use their newly created knowledge to develop an approach to teaching and learning that has impact. We will return to this in Chapter 4.

> **Box 1.3 Achieving cognitive dissonance**
> The aim of the research strips exercise is to create cognitive dissonance (i.e. to perceive information that is contrary to our beliefs). But there are also other ways to achieve this. One approach, for instance, could be to ask PLN participants to read a research review using two different coloured pens: one colour to underline what they do agree with and one colour to underline what they don't agree with. Ensuring that PLN participants consciously think as they read helps avoid ideas 'balkanization' i.e. it ensures we challenge ourselves to be engaged, rather than overlook ideas that challenge our pre-existing world view.

Professional learning task: exploring and applying research literature

We have replicated the research strips exercise, (Box 1.3) in Figure 1.3. As you can see, we have set out a sample of research strips from a literature review on the topic of *assessment for learning*. Why not photocopy this take the strips and cut them up? Working with a colleague, read each strip in turn and agree on a theme it appears to suggest – the strategy or concept or idea the statement on the strip represents. Label this theme using a post-it note. For each strip, either allocate it a new theme or place it within an existing theme. When you have done this for all 12 strips, complete the form below entitled: *Research theme connection to knowledge and practice* (Figure 1.4), which asks you to think about how the research evidence you have just engaged with relates to your existing knowledge on assessment for learning.

Figure 1.3 Example of the RLN research strips exercise

Research Strips

The following statements are a summary of key findings from the following pieces of research literature on *assessment for learning*: Flórez and Sammons (2013), Hattie (2013) and Wiliam et al. (2004).

An assessment activity can help learning if it provides information to be used as feedback by teachers, and by their students in assessing themselves and each other, to modify the teaching and learning activities in which they are engaged. Such assessment becomes 'formative assessment' when the evidence is actually used to adapt the teaching work to meet learning needs.

As an overall factor, feedback has been shown to have one of the biggest effect sizes on student achievement – effective feedback being able to advance a student's achievement by about a year. However, this is based on hundreds of studies and only reveals an overall average finding.

While plenty of research indicates that effective formative feedback approaches lead to increased student attainment, the research is often limited in that it fails to separate out the effect of the feedback from the wider approach within which this was used, for example whole group approaches or direct instruction. This points to the need for teachers to see formative assessment as part of a toolkit of effective strategies, or as a principle that underpins the use of other techniques, such as questioning skills.

Consistent findings have emerged about the importance of questioning style. Most teachers use mainly closed questions which encourage a shallow, surface-level checking of understanding. Greater use of open questions to develop higher-order patterns of thinking are encouraged.

Some research from the area of PE education suggests that models of use in this subject for questioning and feedback may be helpful to use in other areas of the curriculum, such as English and maths. This type of feedback is often rapid, immediate and reciprocal, and students are said to be less likely to respond negatively to criticism due to the way the feedback is delivered.

Much of the emphasis on techniques in feedback concerns feedback that teachers give to students in order to enhance their learning. A range of techniques are used, including: two stars and a wish, now and next steps, traffic lights, comments only, comments linked to criteria, end of lesson review, peer review, progress reports, reflective portfolio comments, computer-generated feedback and the use of rubrics.

Assessment for learning is any assessment for which the first priority in its design and practice is to serve the purpose of promoting students' learning. It thus differs from assessment designed primarily to serve the purposes of accountability, or of ranking, or of certifying competence.

Marking is less helpful when it focuses the student's mind on their positional level relative to other students in the class. This reinforces a performance orientation and can lead to maladaptive learning strategies, such as avoiding practising or trying new learning approaches.

Figure 1.3 Continued

> One major international literature review suggests that feedback either comes from the student to the teacher or from the teacher to the student. This mutually iterative dynamic should inform the whole teaching and learning process. Hattie, the distinguished New Zealand academic, suggests that the important feedback is that which the teacher derives from the student in order to be able to adapt teaching in a suitable way to take learning on a stage further.
>
> Four key areas of research emerge from the literature on AfL: questioning, feedback, peer and self-assessment, the formative use of summative assessment.
>
> Generally, the research shows that comment-only feedback is superior to grade- or mark-only feedback. Feedback needs to be 'informative and descriptive' and should help students show where they are in relation to the learning goals and give strategies and advice on how to bridge the gap.
>
> Teachers need to give greater thinking time once questions have been asked, and greater time should be given for children to respond, in order for students to elaborate and explain their answers. In order to achieve this, a classroom climate conducive to dialogue must be created, where mistakes are welcome and where teachers are seen to be learning from students as well as vice versa.

Figure 1.4 Data capture mat to support the process of knowledge creation

Research theme connection to knowledge and practice

... connects with our own knowledge and practice	... deepens our knowledge and practice	... challenges our knowledge and practice

> **Chapter take-aways**
>
> - PLNs should always commence with a problem that you find yourself unable to tackle alone. But galvanizing support requires others to also see that the problem matters to them. This means PLN participants need to agree on goals focused on concrete outcomes for students.
> - Often such goals will be underpinned by a sense of moral imperative – of doing the best you can for each child. What is helpful, then, is to be specific on what will change for the better if the PLN is a success: this helps create alignment amongst PLN members and the foundation for future action. At the same time, a concrete understanding of the current situation will also be required before any action commences (since this enables us to understand whether impact has occurred).
> - We can also examine what both practitioner-held and research-based knowledge say about the problem in hand and the types of approaches that might help us reach our desired vision for student outcomes. Important, however, is to create cognitive dissonance when engaging with such knowledge types, so as to enable PLN participants to be open to a wide set of ideas and perspectives that may help address the problem in hand.

References

Begley, P. and Johansson, O. (2003) *The Ethical Dimensions of School Leadership*. Dordrecht: Kluwer.

Braunberger, D. and Hamilton, S. (2022) Covid-19 driven emergence of an informal network to support vulnerable students, in G. Handscomb and C. Brown (eds) *The Power of Professional Learning Networks: Traversing the Present; Transforming the Future*. Woodbridge: John Catt, pp. 219–32.

Brown, C. (2018) Research Learning Networks: A case study in using networks to increase knowledge mobilization at scale, in C. Brown and C.L. Poortman (eds) *Networks for Learning: Effective Collaboration for Teacher, School and System Improvement*. London: Routledge, pp. 38–55.

Brown, C. and Rogers, S. (2015) Knowledge creation as an approach to facilitating evidence-informed practice: Examining ways to measure the success of using this method with early years practitioners in Camden (London), *Journal of Educational Change*, 16(1): 79–99.

Cameron, A. and Farrar, M. (2022) Change, adaptation and transformation: Peer review and collaborative improvement during the time of Covid, in G. Handscomb and C. Brown (eds) *The Power of Professional Learning Networks: Traversing the Present; Transforming the Future*. Woodbridge: John Catt, pp. 59–74.

Campbell, C., Lieberman, A. and Yashkina, A. (2016) Developing professional capital in policy and practice, *Journal of Professional Capital and Community*, 1(3): 219–36.

Day, C. and Sammons, P. (2013) *Successful Leadership: A Review of the International Literature*. Reading: CfBT Education Trust.

Earl, L. and Katz, S. (2006) *How Networked Learning Communities Work*, Centre for Strategic Education Seminar Series Paper 155. Melbourne: Centre for Strategic Education.

Flórez, M.T. and Sammons, P. (2013) *Assessment for Learning: Effects and Impact*. London: CfBT.

Fraser, P. and Fulop, G. (2022) Fostering school collaboration across schools around the world: Insights from TALIS, in G. Handscomb and C. Brown (eds) *The Power of Professional Learning Networks: Traversing the Present; Transforming the Future*. Woodbridge: John Catt, pp. 43–58.

Greany, T. and Wolfe, A. (2022) Networking small rural schools in the pandemic, in G. Handscomb and C. Brown (eds) *The Power of Professional Learning Networks: Traversing the Present; Transforming the Future*. Woodbridge: John Catt, pp. 75–90.

Hattie, J. (2013) *Visible Learning: A Synthesis of Over 800 Meta-Analyses Relating to Achievement*. London: Routledge.

Hopkins, D. (2022) The role of networks in supporting school improvement, in G. Handscomb and C. Brown (eds) *The Power of Professional Learning Networks: Traversing the Present; Transforming the Future*. Woodbridge: John Catt.

Nonaka, I. and Takeuchi, H. (1995) *The Knowledge Creating Company: How Japanese Companies Create the Dynamics of Innovation*. New York: Oxford University Press.

Ontario Ministry of Education (n.d.) *Teacher Learning and Leadership Program for Experienced Teachers: Program Guideline*. Toronto, Ontario: Queen's Printer for Ontario.

Poortman, C.L. and Brown, C. (2018) The importance of Professional Learning Networks, in C. Brown and C.L. Poortman (eds) *Networks for Learning: Effective Collaboration for Teacher, School and System Improvement*. London: Routledge, pp. 10–19.

Prenger, R., Poortman, C.L. and Handelzalts, A. (2019) The effects of networked professional learning communities, *Journal of Teacher Education*, 70(5): 441–52.

Schildkamp, K., Poortman, C.L. and Handelzalts, A. (2016) Data teams for school improvement, *School Effectiveness and School Improvement*, 27(2): 228–54.

Stoll, L. and Brown, C. (2015) Middle leaders as catalysts for evidence informed change, in C. Brown (ed.) *Leading the Use of Research and Evidence in Schools*. London: IOE Press.

Stoll, L., Harris, A. and Handscomb, G. (2012) *Great Professional Development that Leads to Great Pedagogy: Nine Strong Claims from Research*. Nottingham: National College for School Leadership.

Strike, K. (2007) *Ethical Leadership in Schools: Creating Community in an Environment of Accountability*. Thousand Oaks, CA: Corwin Press.

Wiliam, D., Lee, C., Harrison, C. and Black, P. (2004) Teachers developing assessment for learning: Impact on student achievement, *Assessment in Education*, 11(1): 49–65.

2 Finding allies when forming a Professional Learning Network

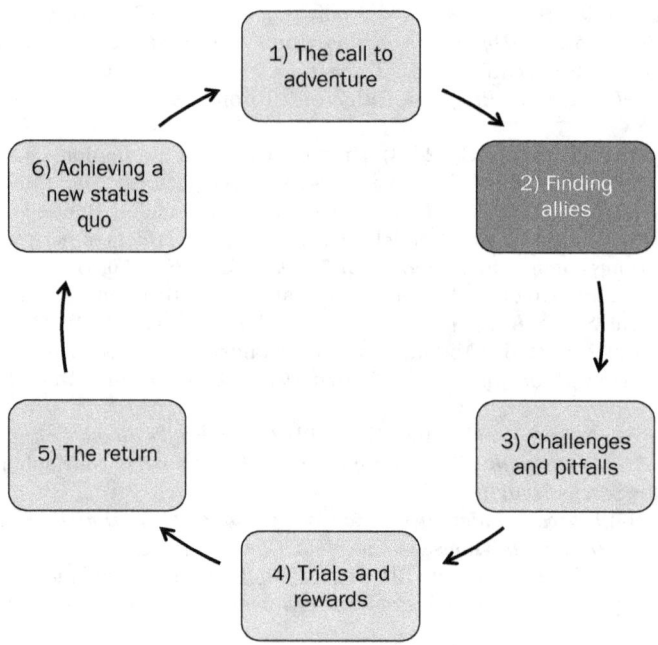

Establishing a PLN is no easy task, and requires us to address a number of issues. For example, we need to consider who we will involve and ascertain what support might be required to enable colleagues to participate effectively. We tackle such issues in this chapter. As we have already highlighted in the introduction to this book, PLNs are concerned with the structured learning of teachers. The aim is that such learning results in positive changes to teaching practice, as well as to student learning and related student outcomes. When we think about teacher learning, however, it is important to recognize that, with PLNs, such learning happens in two distinct ways. First, PLN participants learn as part of the PLN process: through their engagement with other PLN participants and with sources of knowledge including research and data. Second, this learning should then continue back in PLN participants' 'home' schools. In other words, PLN participants need to ensure the process of learning that originates within the PLN continues among their colleagues.

Because PLN-related learning happens in two different ways, however, this means we need to think about: i) who we want to learn with as part of the PLN (in other words, who should be in the room to ensure learning is maximally beneficial); and ii) who might help us ensure that PLN-related learning spreads widely and effectively amongst our colleagues in our 'home' schools. Let's look at this in more detail.

Beyond school expertise and knowledge

As we learned in the previous chapter, often PLNs have a goal of developing context-specific strategies for improvement (Howland, 2015). For instance, networks might have a focus on addressing challenging circumstances and/or persistent issues of inequity and underperformance (i.e. ensuring all students, irrespective of background, gain the minimum skills necessary to function in today's society: Armstrong, 2015; Arkhipenka et al., 2018). Other focus areas can include students' transition from school to work, or pervasive problems such as childhood obesity (Díaz-Gibson et al., 2017). As was also touched upon in the last chapter, it is only by connecting with the best available evidence that educators will be able to identify both the real cause of any problem they are trying to tackle, as well as those approaches most likely to address it.[1] Two good examples of PLNs addressing and tackling issues of teaching and learning via in-depth and reflective engagement are **Research Learning Networks** and **data teams** (see also Chapter 4). In both examples, practitioner expertise and contextual knowledge (including that of students) are combined with the use of academic research and data (see Box 2.1 and Chapters 1 and 4 for more detail on these PLNs and the processes they employ).

> **Box 2.1 Research Learning Networks and data teams**
>
> Research Learning Networks (RLNs) are a specific type of PLN designed to enable the roll-out of new research-informed teaching practice at scale, by engaging teachers in a four-stage cycle of inquiry. Here specific teachers, school leaders and 'opinion-formers' from approximately four to six schools come together to engage with research that relates to a specific teaching and learning issue (for example, improving student metacognition). The schools meet four times a year in whole day workshops, and participating teachers are facilitated by academic researchers to: a) develop research-informed

---

[1] In general, of course, we also see it as a given that teachers should be constantly updating their skills and knowledge if they are to adapt to fast-changing social and economic-related educational imperatives of the modern age.

teaching practices designed to tackle the issue in question; b) trial these new practices in their home schools and evaluate their effectiveness; c) if perceived as successful, roll this strategy out more widely to their colleagues; and d) evaluate and share impact.

In 'data teams' (Schildkamp et al., 2018), meanwhile, PLN participants engage with a variety of data sources (including standardized assessment data, student interview data and observation data) via an eight-step approach that moves from defining problems to developing and evaluating solutions to that problem. More specifically, it involves teachers:

1. defining the problem in hand;
2. developing hypotheses (or research questions) with regard to possible causes of this problem;
3. collecting data;
4. checking the quality of the collected data;
5. analysing and interpreting the data;
6. drawing conclusions about the hypotheses (or research questions);
7. taking action; and
8. evaluating.

At the same time, there are a number of well-acknowledged factors associated with teachers engaging with academic research and data. For instance, educators can often struggle to access academic research, which may often be situated behind paywalls. It can also be hard for educators to engage with academic research due to the specialist nature of the language used (Cain et al., 2019). There has been much critique of the quality of educational research as well as the related suggestion that it should not be trusted to provide a firm basis for practice development (Biesta, 2007; Wisby and Whitty, 2017; Wrigley, 2018). Academic research is also often critiqued either for being too context independent or because it reports on very specific contexts. When it comes to data, educators also need to be data 'literate'. In particular, teachers need to be able to:

1. collect data;
2. appraise the quality of the data;
3. analyse and interpret data;
4. transform data into information, and decisions;
5. implement actions; and
6. evaluate the outcomes of these actions.

Points 1 to 6 above all represent skills that teachers often lack (Brown et al., 2017). To overcome these issues, a partnership approach between schools and universities is suggested (see Box 2.2). This is because when PLNs involve a collaboration between schools and universities, this invariably enables the former to draw on resource(s) – such as knowledge and expertise relating to research and data, as well as sources of research and data. This can subsequently help teachers and schools develop effective educational practices that address challenges which are too complex for isolated institutions to tackle by themselves (see Box 2.2).

> **Box 2.2 Dutch national PLN project**
>
> In a Dutch national PLN project (2013–17), 23 PLNs – each with 10–25 participants from different schools – were charged with developing new lesson materials, developing teachers' research attitude and skills, or attending to both of these things. Participants came together at least monthly for a minimum of 12 months and the PLNs were guided by one or two external coaches from a local university. Coaches supported participants by undertaking different roles: that of content expert, coordinator (e.g. organization and structure of the meetings) and process manager. Vitally, the latter role has been found to be key for ensuring participants' in-depth and reflective engagement within the PLN process.

Involving other schools

Opportunities for learning and collaborative inquiry increase if schools can make use of a wide range of resources and expertise (Stoll, 2010; Prenger et al., 2021). You will have already identified a burning issue or problem (the basis for your quest) in Chapter 1. Given this problem is likely to be faced by lots of other schools, many of which will have interesting ideas on how to tackle it, we are likely to want to form a PLN with other schools facing similar challenges. But do we want to choose schools that are in the same boat as us, or those who have already made headway in tackling the issue? Interestingly, this is actually a question of trust. As you might expect, PLNs work most effectively when there is trust between the participants. But research suggests that trust is likely to materialize more quickly when networking takes place between schools with similar quality features and similar context factors (Bremm and Drucks, 2018). This is the notion of **homogeneous networks** – an approach which contrasts with much of the perceived knowledge of school systems such as in England, where networks often consist of high- and low-achieving schools in order that the latter can learn and benefit from engaging with the former (Chapman and Muijs, 2014; Howland, 2015). An example of a successful approach to establishing homogeneous networks can be found in Box 2.3.

> **Box 2.3 Developing potential learning networks (Germany)**
>
> The *Developing Potential – Empowering Schools* project supports systematic school development processes in 36 secondary schools serving disadvantaged students in the Ruhr metropolis, Germany. Participating schools are set up in school-to-school networks and, using a data-driven approach, the schools engage in one of three networked school development topics: a) 'teacher collaboration and differentiation in heterogeneous groups' (i.e. when students are from different backgrounds and have different abilities); b) 'teaching development'; or c) 'effective use of resources'. Networks meet four times a year over a total period of four years. Schools are additionally supported on an individual basis by a school development coach and via teacher training.

> The aim of the development part of the project is to support schools in building capacities for organizational learning in general, as well as improving those areas of school and teaching quality that have been identified as key development foci (Bremm and Drucks, 2018).

Related, however, is how networks coalesce. There are plenty of good reasons for selecting participating schools based on how geographically 'close' they are to each other. When schools are located near to one another, it makes it easier for participants to physically meet. But it also means there is more likely to be a feeling of shared community, aspirations and needs (especially in relation to demographics) (e.g. Howland, 2015; Tulowitzki et al., 2018). What's more, with a shared geography comes a common history and understanding (Howland, 2015). But harking back to trust, for this to happen effectively, PLNs need to eschew the fear of competition – for example, competition regarding new ideas in terms of attracting students when in adjacent neighbourhoods (Bremm and Drucks, 2018). Rather, participating schools need to jointly pursue a moral imperative of achieving the best for every child within a given district. Moreover, PLNs are substantially influenced by factors such as:

1. school leadership, for example in terms of vision for school improvement in relation to the PLN focus;
2. involving other colleagues;
3. facilitation; and
4. leaders' own active participation in PLN(-related) activities.

These factors need to be taken into account in finding allies (van den Boom-Muilenburg et al., 2022a; Prenger et al., 2022).

Our teaching colleagues

Closer to home, we also need to think about our teacher colleagues (those we work with on a day-to-day basis). Here we need to consider who to involve in the ongoing activities of the PLN and who to co-opt back at our 'home' school. In both cases, it's useful to consider the idea of 'change agents': those individuals, whether inside or outside an organization, who possess the capacity or opportunity to successfully transform aspects of how that organization operates (Fullan, 1993, 2011). In other words, change agents are those people best able to catalyse the successful introduction of innovations or perspectives into one's school. Change agents are increasingly viewed as vital to the successful operation of schools and school systems. For instance, in 'self-improving' school systems, such as in England, Ontario and New South Wales, improvements in children's outcomes are positioned as occurring when teachers mobilize innovations, practices, perspectives and ideas (collectively described as 'new ways of working') amongst colleagues (Ainscow, 2014; Greany and Higham, 2018). As these new ways of working are adopted, the attitudes and practices of teachers and other practitioners change, ideally resulting in improvements in student outcomes (academic or otherwise: Earley and Greany, 2017). When such improvement occurs in disadvantaged areas, it can also lead to reductions in the gap in education outcomes between students from the most and least affluent families (Brown, 2020).

As we intimated in the introduction to this book, in self-improving school systems the mobilization of new ways of working is undertaken by teachers and informal leaders as well as formal school leaders (Kotter, 2014; Wenner and Campbell, 2017). Yet not all teachers are equal in their ability to mobilize new ways of working, such that they are adopted widely. Understanding which teachers are best able to encourage the take-up of new ways of working is therefore vital to ensuring that what you do in your PLN makes a difference. In other words, that you are able to continuously improve the education children receive, as well as improving equity in student achievement. So, who makes an effective educational change agent? First, we need to consider whether the change agents in question will be joining you on your quest and participating fully in the PLN or whether they are those who you need to work with outside of the PLN to ensure change happens.

Let's start with who might join you on your PLN journey. Here, a number of studies provide us with useful insight. For example, when viewed through the lens of social network theory, the success or failure of educational change is dependent on the social networks through which it is mediated (Coburn et al., 2010; Warren Little, 2010; van den Boom-Muilenburg et al., 2022b). A social network represents a set of relevant actors (persons or groups) connected to each other by a specific type of relationship, which enables individuals to access a range of social capital resources (Daly, 2010). For instance, 'instrumental' social capital resources such as information-sharing, advice-giving and problem-solving provide concrete support for achieving specific goals. In contrast, 'expressive' social capital refers to resources such as trust, support and encouragement, all of which can influence attitudes towards given goals and instil the resilience required to keep pursuing them (Puccia et al., 2021). From this perspective, change agents will be those individuals best situated within a social network to mobilize both types of social capital in support of a given change (Finnigan and Daly, 2010; Battilana and Casciaro, 2013). See Box 2.4 for how you might identify change agents in your school.

Box 2.4 Identifying change agents

The following exercise can be used to think about how knowledge flows around your school. To begin with, take a sheet of A3 paper. Then allocate different shapes for different roles within your school. For example, circles could represent those in senior leadership positions, triangles could represent middle leaders and stars could represent teachers. Colour can be used to delineate

22 The Teacher's Guide to Professional Learning Networks

teams, e.g. year groups or departments. Thinking of the question, 'to whom do teachers turn as reliable sources of expertise in terms of teaching and learning?', draw lines and arrows to show how knowledge flows within your school. Does this change when thinking about expressive forms of social capital (such as advice-giving)? What does this tell you about who should be involved in your PLN journey?

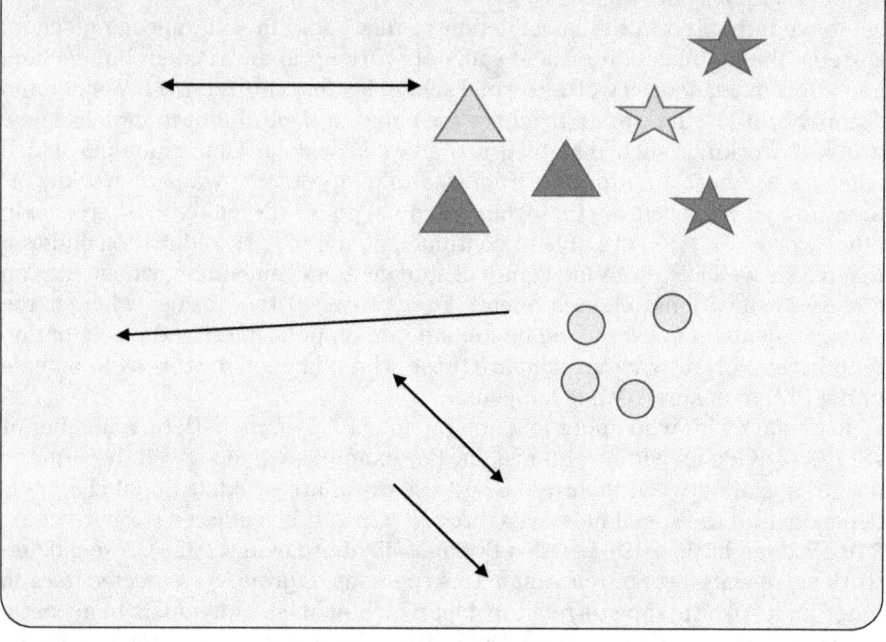

From another perspective (that of 'organizational semiotics': e.g. Gazendam et al., 2003), effective change agents are those who are best able to signal that a specific change is attractive enough for others to adopt. In this sense, 'attractiveness' can refer to the idea represented by the change in question, but it can also represent the extent to which an idea appears *achievable*; in other words, whether those expected to change believe they possess the ability to successfully pursue it. As with any form of semiotic, a 'thing' (an object or idea) only has meaning when viewed in relation to other 'things' (Eco, 1979). A change agent can therefore position a change as attractive by contrasting it with something that teachers regard as less attractive. For example, Schildkamp and Datnow (2022) observe that teachers are far *more* likely to consider using data to inform their practice when there is an explicit focus on equity, than when data use is undertaken in the service of accountability. The achievability of the change therefore involves change agents signalling certain attributes of the change in question – for instance, how easy a change is to master, and/or the extent to which it involves changers drawing on familiar sets of skills and practices (Rogers, 1995).

There are also psychological perspectives that add insight; specifically the concept of heuristics (Tversky and Kahneman, 1974; Kahneman, 2011). One common heuristic is homophily: the conscious or unconscious tendency to associate with people 'like ourselves' (Daly, 2010). There is some debate as to whether homophily is an objective preference, however, and further insight here is provided in Box 2.5, as well as detail on some other types of heuristics to be aware of. In summary, what the heuristic perspective suggests is that change agents are those most able to galvanize change because they are viewed as being acceptable to follow: they are seen as being 'like me'; as possessing admirable qualities; likely to be charismatic; connected to 'others whom I like'. The most effective change agents are therefore those that others gravitate towards.

Box 2.5 Homophily and other heuristics

Homophily is the idea that like attracts like or, as it's more commonly expressed, that 'birds of a feather flock together'. The notion of homophily can be found as far back as ancient Greece, where Socrates is reported to have suggested that 'similarity begets friendship', and as such, we should 'delight in equals'; Aristotle likewise observed that we tend to 'love those who are like ourselves'. But as a phenomenon, our tendency to interact with others who are like us was only formally coined as homophily by Paul Lazarsfeld and Robert Merton in 1954, the etymology of the word deriving from the combination of two ancient Greek words: homo – the same – and phily – liking. Intuitively, the concept seems to be right. Think about it for a moment; of your closest connections or core friends, how many are from the same ethnic background as you, or the same social class? How many have a similar educational background?

But is homophily really an objective preference? Some scientists are now beginning to think that it's not; suggesting, for instance, that if person A possesses a quality that person B particularly likes or admires, such as high levels of subject or pedagogic knowledge, B will transform their view of A, projecting feelings of similarity and so 'tricking themselves' that commonality exists (Weller and Watson, 2009). Similarly, if person A impresses person B, person B may ascribe this to a quality they believe they themselves possess. Whether real or perceived, however, if two people believe they are alike, they are more likely to enter into a relationship than if they believe they are significantly different.

Other identified heuristics affecting how people perceive one another include the *reputation heuristic* and the *popularity effect*. With the former, people are 'judged' based on their known relationships, leading to a number of simple but well understood maxims that guide who to connect with – for instance, that 'a friend of my friend is a friend' or that 'an enemy of my enemy is a friend' (Gross and De Dreu, 2019). The latter suggests that when people see others start connecting with an individual, they will do so too – so explaining why popular individuals tend to become ever more popular (Topirceanu et al., 2018).

These three lenses – the social network, the semiotic and the heuristic – are most useful when considering change agents as those attempting to influence an organization *from the bottom up*. In other words, they can help you identify who you might want with you as part of the PLN activity. Further attributes of effective 'bottom-up' change agents are that:

1. They display **agency**: they evaluate need and activate change through a collaborative process that attends to the motivation of others (Lukacs and Galluzzo, 2014; Lai and Cheung, 2015; Wenner and Campbell, 2017).
2. They display **cultural competence**: bottom-up change agents are aware of the sociocultural context they operate in, have high expectations, a desire to make a difference, and are cognisant of the need to challenge the deficit mindset of colleagues. This type of change leader may also identify means through which to overcome the professional antinomies (contradictions) often faced by teachers working in disadvantaged and challenging situations, including drawing on those holding 'local knowledge', such as that of teaching assistants (Hauge et al., 2014; Von Hippel, 2014; Lee and Louis, 2019).
3. They are **effective relationship builders** with colleagues within their school, and also externally: bottom-up change agents engage with key local stakeholders (parents, community groups and so forth) to co-construct the difference they are seeking to achieve and the means of achieving it (Poekert et al., 2016; Schnellert, 2020).

Co-opting teachers in your 'home' school

You may also want to find other allies back in your school to support you in your change endeavours. This second group of allies might not take part in the PLN itself, but they will be instrumental in helping you spread new ideas and innovations to everyone in your school. To work out who might support you most effectively here, we can examine what we currently know about which teachers are best placed to lead *top-down* change. In other words, when the nature of the change in question has more or less already been determined by school leaders, higher-level (local or central) policymakers, or indeed you and the work you and colleagues have undertaken as part of your PLN. An in-depth review of this area (undertaken by Brown et al., 2021) suggests that choosing 'top-down' change agents based on their possession of specific qualities can be effective – with examples of such qualities, including:

1. **Attitudes to change** generally or to a particular change, including knowledge, beliefs and values (Fullan, 2011; Lai and Cheung, 2015; Poekert et al., 2016).
2. **Mastery of subject knowledge** and/or pedagogy; for instance, whether they possess expertise, which in itself was viewed as a function of years of experience and perceived subject knowledge (Booth et al., 2021).

3 Whether the change agent is a **lifelong learner**: someone who is curious, open minded or has a growth mindset and is willing to try new approaches (Ali, 2011; Schleicher, 2012; Watson, 2014; Beauchamp, 2015).
4 Whether the change agent has **entrepreneurial qualities**: for instance, whether they are happy to take risks to see if a change can be enhanced further. And similarly, whether they can encourage others to do the same (Kools and Stoll, 2016; Wenner and Campbell, 2017).
5 Whether the change agent is an **effective collaborator**, with strong collegial standing, and someone who can leverage their networks effectively to help secure change (Daly, 2010; Warren Little, 2010; Battilana and Casciaro, 2013; Hairon and Goh, 2015; van der Heijden et al., 2015; Doğan and Adams, 2018).

Other tools and methods for identifying both bottom-up and top-down change agents can be found in Box 2.6, and these can be used to see who in your school is most likely to help you facilitate change.

Box 2.6 Ways to identify change agents

A recent review of change agents by Brown and colleagues (2021) revealed a number of tools, methods and approaches developed to identify change agents. These include:

1 **Actualized Leadership Profile:** this is a brief exercise for school leaders to select one descriptive word from each of ten word-pairs that they feel best depicts their professional style: https://alpfree.com
2 Mid-continent for Research Education and Learning's **Balanced Leadership Profile®:** a research-informed 'profile' that depicts 21 leadership responsibilities that have significant correlations with student achievement.
3 **Teacher Change Agent Scale:** this is a 15-item Likert-style scale designed to measure teachers' willingness to be change agents.
4 **Social network theory and social network analysis:** previously used in studies (e.g. Rose et al., 2017) as a way of identifying 'opinion-formers' who take part in a specific-change intervention. Here, opinion-formers were defined as those with the highest levels of 'in-degree' centrality in their school's advice and support network. In other words, they were the people most often turned to for advice and support by colleagues.

We can also consider what allies we might co-opt by thinking about the roles they will undertake. Here, research by Lai and Cheung (2015) suggests the following six roles are involved in introducing top-down change:

1 Interacting with other school members around school reform efforts.
2 Striving for pedagogical excellence.
3 Confronting barriers in the school's culture and structures.
4 Translating ideas into actions.

5 Participating in decision-making.
6 Taking the initiative in leading school improvement.

Lai and Cheung go on to argue that in performing these roles, top-down change agents often attempt to achieve three goals:

1 to encourage others to improve their professional practice;
2 to nurture a culture of success; and
3 to continuously demonstrate professionalism (i.e. 'walk the talk').

In a similar vein, there are three broadly conceived means through which your allies might effectively support top-down change:

1 by maintaining focus on teaching and learning;
2 by establishing trusting and constructive relationships; and
3 by interacting through formal and informal points of influence.

So again, who you select needs to be capable of achieving these goals and tasks. At the same time, however, current research fails to articulate the specific actions and tactics that top-down change agents should adopt as they engage in those relationships and interactions, so as to effectively change the pedagogy of other teachers. Research into distributed leadership (e.g. Brown et al., 2020; van den Boom-Muilenburg et al., 2022b), though, indicates that distributed leaders can work effectively as agents of change when they lead processes of professional inquiry as part of 'in-school' professional learning communities. Specifically, distributed leaders can be effective when they attempt to:

1 introduce change by guiding their colleagues to explore specific issues of teaching and learning;
2 introduce colleagues to new ideas relating to specific problems of teaching and learning;
3 support colleagues to test out these new ideas in risk-free environments; and
4 invite colleagues to consider the impact of new approaches to teaching and learning and how they can be refined, augmented and incorporated into existing practice.

We will return in more detail to these practices in Chapter 5 (and consider the notion of distributed leadership in more detail in Chapter 6).

What support do change agents need?

Yet even when you identify change agents to support you, there are a number of factors that can enable or inhibit a change agent's ability to succeed. These include: i) principal or school leadership support; ii) buy-in to the change agent role by practitioner colleagues; iii) access to training and professional development; and iv) perceived autonomy and the change agent's own positioning in the role (Poekert et al., 2016). To begin with, school leaders can show acknowledgement and recognition of teachers' roles as change agents by providing them with classroom release time to work with colleagues, remuneration for the role, or other organizational support such as timetabling in a way to enable them to observe and support colleagues (Brown and Flood, 2019). A lack of time or structural resourcing was noted as a major barrier to a change agent's work, especially since their work is likely to be additional to already busy teaching workloads (Brown and Flood, 2019; Brown, 2020). In terms of the second factor, teacher resistance to change can make teachers' work as change agents difficult, and a perceived lack of support from school leaders can fuel such resistance (Brown et al., 2021). Again, school leaders can provide assistance here, since a shared vision for change can help a change agent's positioning in the eyes of staff members (Brown et al., 2021).

There seems to be little preparation and training afforded to teachers to act as change agents. Programmes vary widely from conferences, centralized professional development and local training courses to university master's degrees (Wenner and Campbell, 2017). Findings from a rapid literature review undertaken by Booth et al. (2021) suggest that 'second stage' teachers (defined as those with three to ten years' experience) who take on 'reform' roles (roles which involve attempting to change the practice of colleagues) generally benefit from two forms of professional development. The first type is that which helps them promote their role, especially when norms exist within schools regarding teacher autonomy, and respect tends to be reserved for those with the highest levels of experience and seniority. The second form of professional development is that designed to support change agents when they encounter resistance to change in their context. Change agents' own perceptions of their role, and their autonomy to act, can either support or hinder them in fulfilling their mission. The change agent's role is often perceived as blurring the line between teaching and leadership in schools, and research has found that, as such, teachers can struggle to define and identify with it (Poekert et al., 2016).

Furthermore, the process evaluation of the Research Learning Network intervention (Rose et al., 2017), where opinion-formers were used as change agents, found that staff turnover, competing priorities and limited time of teachers were barriers to the successful implementation of change, echoing some of the issues noted above. This was because opinion-formers needed to be able to commit to the full duration of the PLN, attend all the workshops, and have time in school to develop their ideas and discuss the project with colleagues. Similarly, work undertaken by Brown and Flood (2019) indicates that if distributed leaders are to be effective change agents, then school leaders need to attend to three areas. First, school leaders need to ensure that distributed leadership activity is formally linked to the policies and processes of the school (such as school improvement plans). Doing so signals its importance, and positions such activity as something that is key to a school's culture and way of working. Second, they need to create the time and space for distributed leaders to interact with colleagues, thus enabling new ideas to be mobilized. Third, they need to help distributed leaders understand how best to mobilize new ideas. This is particularly important, given that our current understanding indicates that the passive dissemination of new ideas and practices is ineffective, while the most impactful forms of mobilization involve school staff actually and collaboratively engaging with innovations. Again, more on distributed leadership and the idea of innovation 'mobilization' will be presented in Chapter 5.

Chapter take-aways

- Many PLNs operate on the basis that the most effective way for teachers to address and tackle issues of teaching and learning is via an in-depth and reflective engagement with academic research and data. Here a partnership between schools and universities enables PLN participants to draw on resources (such as knowledge and expertise relating to research and data, as well as sources of research and data) that can help them develop effective educational practices.
- PLNs also often involve practitioners from schools facing similar circumstances. This works best when participating schools have similar levels of attainment, operate in similar contexts and have shared histories. When geographically proximal, PLN members need to put aside competition for students and instead pursue a moral imperative of achieving the best for every child within a given district.
- Also vital is how change agents are identified and involved: not only those individuals who will be joining you on your quest, but also those who you need to work with in your 'home school' to ensure change happens. But successfully utilizing change agents requires school leader support; buy-in to their role from colleagues; access to training and professional development; and the change agent having a sense of self-efficacy with regard to their role.

References

Ainscow, M. (2014) *Towards Self-Improving School Systems: Lessons from a City Challenge*. London: Routledge.

Ali, T. (2011) Understanding the evolving roles of improvement-oriented high school teachers in Gilgit-Baltistan, *Qualitative Report*, 16(6): 1616–44.

Arkhipenka, V., Dawson, S., Fitriyah, S., Goldrick, S., Howes, A. and Palacios, N. (2018) Practice and performance: Changing perspectives of teachers through collaborative enquiry, *Educational Research*, 60(1): 97–112.

Armstrong, P. (2015) *Effective Partnerships and Collaboration for School Improvement: A Review of the Evidence*. London: Department for Education.

Battilana, J. and Casciaro, T. (2013) The network secrets of great change agents, *Harvard Business Review*, 91(7–8): 62–8.

Beauchamp, C. (2015) Reflection in teacher education: Issues emerging from a review of current literature, *Reflective Practice*, 16(1): 123–41.

Biesta, G. (2007) Why 'what works' won't work: Evidence-based practice and the democratic deficit in educational research, *Educational Theory*, 57(1): 1–22.

Booth, J., Coldwell, M., Müller, L.-M., Perry, E. and Zuccollo, J. (2021) Mid-career teachers: A mixed methods scoping study of professional development, career progression and retention, *Education Sciences*, 11(6): 299. Available at https://doi.org/10.3390/educsci11060299 (accessed 4 November 2022).

Bremm, N. and Drucks, S. (2018) Building up school to school networks using an evidence-based approach. Presented at the European Conference on Educational Research annual meeting, Bolzano (Italy), 4–7 September.

Brown, C. (2020) *The Networked School Leader: How to Improve Teaching and Student Outcomes using Learning Networks.* Bingley: Emerald.

Brown, C. and Flood, J. (2019) *Formalise, Prioritise and Mobilise: How School Leaders Secure the Benefits of Professional Learning Networks.* London: Emerald.

Brown, C., MacGregor, S. and Flood, J. (2020) Can models of distributed leadership be used to mobilise networked generated innovation in schools? A case study from England, *Teaching and Teacher Education*, 94(1), early online access. Available at https://doi.org/10.1016/j.tate.2020.103101 (accessed 4 November 2022).

Brown, C. and Poortman, C. (2018) *Networks for Learning: Effective Collaboration for Teacher, School and System Improvement.* London: Routledge.

Brown, C., Schildkamp, K. and Hubers, M. (2017) Combining the best of two worlds: A conceptual proposal for evidence-informed school improvement, *Educational Research*, 59(2): 154–72.

Brown, C., White, R. and Kelly, A. (2021) Teachers as educational change agents: What do we currently know? Findings from a systematic review, *Emerald Open Research*. Available at https://doi.org/10.35241/emeraldopenres.14385.1 (accessed 4 November 2022).

Cain, T., Brindley, S., Brown, C., Jones, G. and Riga, F. (2019) Bounded decision-making, teachers' reflection, and organisational learning: How research can inform teachers and teaching, *British Educational Research Journal*, 45(5): 1072–87.

Chapman, C. and Muijs, D. (2014) Does school-to-school collaboration promote school improvement? A study of the impact of school federations on student outcomes, *School Effectiveness and School Improvement*, 25(3): 351–93.

Coburn, C., Choi, L. and Mata, W. (2010) 'I would go to her because her mind is math'. Network formation in the context of a district-based mathematics reform, in A. Daly (ed.) *Social Network Theory and Educational Change.* Cambridge, MA: Harvard Education Press, pp. 33–50.

Daly, A. (2010) Mapping the terrain: Social network theory and educational change, in A. Daly (ed.) *Social Network Theory and Educational Change.* Cambridge, MA: Harvard Education Press, pp. 1–16.

Díaz-Gibson, J., Zaragoza, M.C., Daly, A.J., Mayayo, M.J. and Romaní, J.R. (2017) Networked leadership in Educational Collaborative Networks, *Educational Management Administration & Leadership*, 45(6): 1040–59.

Doğan, S. and Adams, A. (2018) Effect of professional learning communities on teachers and students: Reporting updated results and raising questions about research design, *School Effectiveness and School Improvement*, 29(4): 634–59.

Earley, P. and Greany, T. (2017) The future of leadership, in P. Earley and T. Greany (eds) *School Leadership and System Reform in the 21st Century.* London: Bloomsbury, pp. 1–14.

Eco, U. (1979) *A Theory of Semiotics.* Bloomington, IN: Indiana University Press.

Finnigan, K. and Daly, A. (2010) Learning at a system level, in A. Daly (ed.) *Social Network Theory and Educational Change*. Cambridge, MA: Harvard Education Press, pp. 179–96.

Fullan, M. (1993) Why teachers must become change agents, *Educational Leadership*, 50(6): 12–17.

Fullan, M. (2011) *Change Leader: Learning to do what Matters Most*. San Francisco, CA: Jossey-Bass/Wiley.

Gazendam, H., Jorna, R. and Cijsouw, R. (2003) *Dynamics and Change in Organizations: Studies in Organizational Semiotics*. Dordrecht: Springer.

Greany, T. and Higham, R. (2018) *Hierarchy, Markets and Networks: Analysing the 'self-improving school-led system' agenda in England and the implications for schools*. London: UCL IOE Press.

Gross, K. and De Dreu, C. (2019) The rise and fall of cooperation through reputation and group polarization, *Nature Communications*, 10(1): 776. Available at https://doi.org/10.1038/s41467-019-08727-8 (accessed 4 November 2022).

Hairon, S. and Goh, J. (2015) Pursuing the elusive construct of distributed leadership: Is this search over?, *Educational Management & Leadership*, 43(5): 693–718. Available at https://doi.org/10.1177/1741143214535745 (accessed 4 November 2022).

Hauge, T.E., Norenes, S.O. and Vedøy, G. (2014) School leadership and educational change: Tools and practices in shared school leadership development, *Journal of Educational Change*, 15(4): 357–76. Available at https://doi.org/10.1007/s10833-014-9228-y (accessed 4 November 2022).

Howland, G. (2015) Structural reform: The experience of ten schools driving the development of an all-age hard federation across a market town in northern England, *Management in Education*, 29(1): 25–30.

Kahneman, D. (2011) *Thinking, Fast and Slow*. London: Allen Lane.

Kools, M. and Stoll, L. (2016) *What Makes a School a Learning Organisation?*, OECD Education Working Papers, No. 137. Paris: OECD Publishing. Available at https://doi.org/10.1787/5jlwm62b3bvh-en.

Kotter, J. (2014) *Accelerate: Building Strategic Agility for a Faster-Moving World*. Cambridge, MA: Harvard Business School Press.

Lai, E. and Cheung, D. (2015) Enacting teacher leadership: The role of teachers in bringing about change, *Educational Management Administration & Leadership*, 43(5): 673–92.

Lee, M. and Louis, K.S. (2019) Mapping a strong school culture and linking it to sustainable school improvement, *Teaching and Teacher Education*, 81: 84–96. Available at https://doi.org/10.1016/j.tate.2019.02.001 (accessed 4 November 2022).

Lukacs, K.S. and Galluzzo, G.R. (2014) Beyond empty vessels and bridges: Toward defining teachers as the agents of school change, *Teacher Development*, 18(1): 100–6.

Poekert, P., Alexandrou, A. and Shannon, D. (2016) How teachers become leaders: An internationally validated theoretical model of teacher leadership development, *Research in Post-Compulsory Education*, 21(4): 307–29.

Prenger, R., Poortman, C.L. and Handelzalts, A. (2021) Professional Learning Networks: From teacher learning to school improvement?, *Journal of Educational Change*, 22(1): 13–52.

Prenger, R., Tappel, A.P.M., Poortman, C.L. and Schildkamp, K. (2022) How can educational innovations become sustainable? A review of the empirical literature, *Frontiers in Education*, 7: 970715. Available at https://doi.org/10.3389/feduc.2022.970715.

Puccia, E., Martin, J.P., Smith, C.A.S. et al. (2021) The influence of expressive and instrumental social capital from parents on women and underrepresented minority students' declaration and persistence in engineering majors, *International Journal of STEM Education*, 8: 20. Available at https://doi.org/10.1186/s40594-021-00277-0 (accessed 4 November 2022).

Rose, J., Thomas, S., Zhang, L., Edwards, A., Augero, A. and Rooney, P. (2017) *Research Learning Communities Evaluation Report and Executive Summary: December 2017*. London: Education Endowment Foundation. Available at https://educationendowmentfoundation.org.uk/public/files/Projects/Evaluation_Reports/Research_Learning_Communities.pdf (accessed 11 November 2022).

Schildkamp, K. and Datnow, A. (2022) When data teams struggle: Learning from less successful data use efforts, *Leadership and Policy in Schools*, 21(2): 147–66. Available at https://doi.org/10.1080/15700763.2020.1734630 (accessed 4 November 2022).

Schleicher, A. (2012) *Preparing Teachers and Developing School Leaders for the 21st Century: Lessons from Around the World*. Paris: OECD Publishing.

Schnellert, L. (2020) *Professional Learning Networks: Facilitating Transformation in Diverse Contexts with Equity-Seeking Communities*. Bingley: Emerald.

Stoll, L. (2010) Connecting learning communities: Capacity building for systemic change, in A. Hargreaves, A. Lieberman, M. Fullan and D. Hopkins (eds) *Second International Handbook of Educational Change*. Dordrecht: Springer, pp. 469–84.

Topirceanu, A., Udrescu, M. and Marculescu, R. (2018) Weighted betweenness preferential attachment: A new mechanism explaining social network formation and evolution, *Scientific Reports*, 8(1): 10871. Available at https://doi.org/10.1038/s41598-018-29224-w (accessed 4 November 2022).

Tulowitzki, P., Duveneck, A. and Krüger, M. (2018) A Professional Learning Network for the entire local education system: Educational landscapes in Germany, in C. Brown and C. Poortman (eds) *Networks for Learning: Effective Collaboration for Teacher, School and System Improvement*. London: Routledge, pp. 115–34.

Tversky, A. and Kahneman, D. (1974) Judgment under uncertainty: Heuristics and biases, *Science*, 185(4157): 1124–31.

Van den Boom-Muilenburg, S.N. (2021) The role of school leadership in schools that work sustainably on school improvement with professional learning communities. Dissertation, University of Twente, Enschede.

Van den Boom-Muilenburg, S.N., de Vries, S., van Veen, K., Poortman, C. and Schildkamp, K. (2022a) Leadership practices and sustained lesson study, *Educational Research*, 64(3): 295–316.

Van den Boom-Muilenburg, S.N., Poortman, C.L., Daly, A.J. et al. (2022b) Key actors leading knowledge brokerage for sustainable school improvement with PLCs: Who brokers what?, *Teaching and Teacher Education*, 110(3): 103577.

Van der Heijden, H.R.M.A., Geldens, J.J.M., Beijaard, D. and Popeijus, H.L. (2015) Characteristics of teachers as change agents, *Teachers and Teaching*, 21(6): 681–99. Available at http://doi.org/10.1080/13540602.2015.1044328 (accessed 4 November 2022).

Von Hippel, A. (2014) Program planning caught between heterogeneous expectations – an approach to the differentiation of contradictory constellations and professional antinomies, *Edukacja Dorosłych*, 1(70): 169–84.

Warren Little, J. (2010) Foreword, in A. Daly (ed.) *Social Network Theory and Educational Change*. Cambridge, MA: Harvard Education Press, pp. xi–xiv.

Watson, C. (2014) Effective professional learning communities? The possibilities for teachers as agents of change in schools, *British Educational Research Journal*, 40(1): 18–29.

Weller, J. and Watson, D. (2009) Friend or foe? Differential use of the self-based heuristic as a function of relationship satisfaction, *Journal of Personality*, 27(3): 731–60.

Wenner, J.A. and Campbell, T. (2017) The theoretical and empirical basis of teacher leadership: A review of the literature, *Review of Educational Research*, 87(1): 134–71. Available at https://doi.org/10.3102/0034654316653478 (accessed 4 November 2022).

Wisby, E. and Whitty, G. (2017) Is evidence-informed practice any more feasible than evidence-informed policy? Presented at the British Educational Research Association annual conference, Sussex, 5–7 September.

Wrigley, T. (2018) The power of 'evidence': Reliable science or a set of blunt tools?, *British Educational Research Journal*, 44(3): 359–76.

3 | Challenges and pitfalls – successfully running and sustaining your PLN

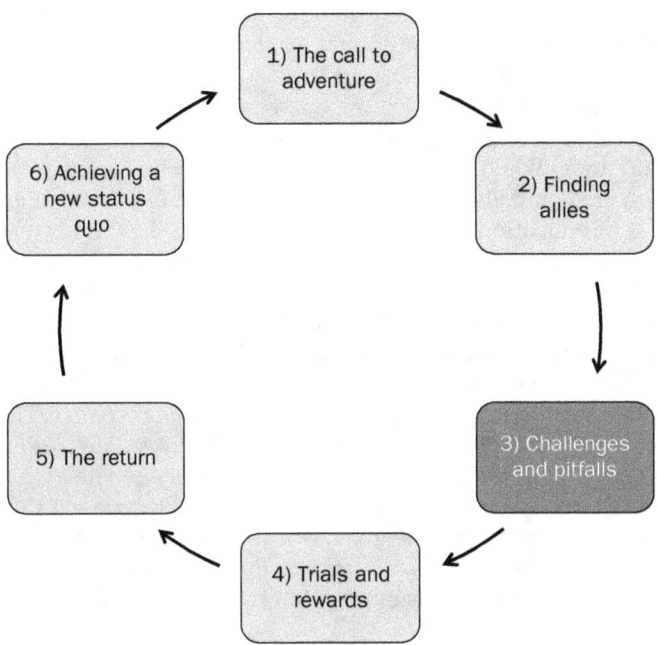

PLNs require a number of conditions to be successful. These include:

1 a shared sense of purpose, centred on student learning;
2 effective collaboration;
3 a spirit of trust and mutual dependence;
4 commitment to reflective inquiry; and
5 effective leadership.

On a practical level, networks also need effective facilitation and an intentional commitment of resources. And they also, of course, need to sustain until the problem they are intended to tackle is resolved. In this chapter, we will address all of these issues (and more) as well as provide practical advice, guidance and tools to help you ensure your PLN lasts the course.

A shared sense of purpose

Although a fundamental part of what we covered in Chapter 1, it's worth restating that PLNs need to possess a **shared sense of purpose and to explore clearly defined and mutually agreed topics** (Rempe-Gillen, 2018; Cameron and Farrar, 2022). While not every member of a PLN needs to share exactly the same goal or reason for participating in the network, there should at least be a set of basic priorities or principles that serve to guide participants. The more participants' goals are aligned and the more PLN members agree on the reasons why they are working together, the easier it will be to maintain a conducive and productive environment and to ensure everyone's expectations are met (Hubers and Poortman, 2018). At the same time, of course, there should also be flexibility to enable the PLN to adapt and so address any new demands or issues that arise. While this common focus should be firmly centred on student learning, it should also be grounded in a mutual understanding regarding the purposes of education – for example, in terms of the values teachers hold *vis-à-vis* the tension that often exists between a focus on performance and instrumental exam outputs versus the role of teachers in providing support for more affective aspects of students' lives. Should views here be fundamentally different, the network may ultimately find itself pulling in different directions in terms of the issues of teaching and learning that need to be addressed, and the appropriate learning and action that should occur in response. This common focus also needs to be both realistic and achievable given the resources available to the network. In a similar vein, network participants need to experience **mutual benefit** from engaging: collaboration is unlikely to last if PLN members believe they can achieve the same goals working as individual schools (Warren Little, 1990; Muijs, 2015). Interim and externally validated short-term 'wins' can often therefore be key to a more long-lasting engagement (Muijs, 2015).

Strong modes of collaboration

PLNs function through establishing networks of formal relationships (between schools, hospitals, agencies, etc.) and informal relationships (e.g. one-to-one social interactions), thereby creating an interconnected approach to tackling important and persistent educational issues (Díaz-Gibson et al., 2017). The diversity of knowledge, skills and capacities that each network participant provides represents an important 'organizational asset', which can be made available to others (Díaz-Gibson et al., 2017: 1043). But only types of collaboration that enable the social capital available within networks to be harnessed will ensure that PLNs function effectively. At a cross-school level such collaboration is dependent on both: i) the coordination of school and school system-level strategies and policies that potentially impact on collaboration; and ii) the adequate provision of resources (in particular time and financial resources) to enable collaboration to occur (Armstrong and Brown, 2022).

Collaboration within networks, meanwhile, requires the inducement of mutual obligation, the fostering of interdependence, the opening up of teacher practice to the scrutiny of others, and encouraging initiative in terms of developing approaches to teaching and learning (Cameron and Farrar, 2022; Fraser and Fulop, 2022). For instance, Warren Little posits four ideal types of collaboration which differ according to the extent to which they induce these key factors: **storytelling and scanning**; **aid and assistance**; **sharing**; and **joint work**. The first, *storytelling*, represents the occasional and opportunistic forays undertaken by teachers as they seek out specific ideas, information, solutions or reassurances. At the same time, teachers remain autonomous and free to choose which of these stories they engage with or act on. In this mode of collaboration, independent trial and error acts as the principal route to developing competence (Warren Little, 1990: 514).

The second ideal type, *aid and assistance*, reflects the idea that teachers offer help and support when asked, but only when asked. This is because, in schools where this mode of collaboration is prevalent, discussions about teaching practice become associated with judgements on the competence of teachers: both judgements about those seeking support and judgements relating to the competency of those supplying such support (Warren Little, 1990: 516). Warren Little's third type of collegiality – *sharing* – spotlights the routine exchange of materials and methods as well as the open interchange of ideas and opinions (1990: 518). Acting in this way provides teachers with an opportunity to learn about others' practices and to compare these to their own. Even so, sharing can be variable in nature: different teachers may engage with more or fewer teachers, their engagement may be fully or only partially reciprocated and teachers may reveal much or little of their thinking, ideas, practice or materials (1990: 518). Warren Little uses the fourth term – *joint work* – to represent encounters among teachers that are grounded in 'shared responsibility for the work of teaching (interdependence), collective conceptions of autonomy, support for teachers' initiative and leadership with regard to professional practice, and group affiliations grounded in professional work' (1990: 519). Teachers are more motivated to collaborate with one another when the success of their efforts depends on it, and as a result of this interdependence, a norm based on the thoughtful, explicit examination of practices and their consequences is likely to emerge (1990: 522).

Naturally, effective collaboration as a face-to-face activity has been greatly impacted by the recent Covid-19 pandemic (Fraser and Fulop, 2022). As we highlighted earlier, however, the pandemic has also facilitated the emergence of digital PLNs. As a result, this has enabled new forms of in-depth joint work to occur. But rather than just collaborating synchronously, a virtual approach has meant that effective collaboration can also occur asynchronously, use novel online collaborative tools, and involve people separated by greater geographic distances than before (Cameron and Farrar, 2022). An online approach is also better for the environment (in terms of carbon footprint) and is relatively low cost compared to meeting face to face, both in terms of travel and time. Of course, when building connections for the first time, many of us would agree that face to face is best. But in a world where people are now used to platforms such as Zoom and Teams, effective online collaboration, situated in between those face-to-face gatherings, is now regarded by many as both doable and natural.

Bringing joint work to life

The notion of Joint Practice Development (JPD) presents another way to consider Warren Little's idea of *joint work*. JPD refers to situations in which teachers, or other educators, use collaborative engagement to develop ways of working that are both shared and examined in depth (Fielding et al., 2005). The JPD process is regarded as effective because it is truly mutual, rather than one-way, and because there is a focus on practice being improved rather than simply moved from one person or place to another (Fielding et al., 2005; Dudley, 2011; Sebba et al., 2012). One popular mode of JPD is Lesson Study, a now globally popular approach to educational improvement. Further detail on the Lesson Study approach is set out in Box 3.1.

> **Box 3.1 What is Lesson Study?**
> Usually described as a 'teaching improvement process', Lesson Study has its origins in Japanese elementary education, where it is a widely used professional development practice (Dudley, 2014; Cheung and Wong, 2014). As a process, Lesson Study involves teachers collaborating, normally in groups of three, to progress cycles of iterative practice development. Such cycles typically involve the following steps: 1) a discussion of student learning goals and the identification of a teaching strategy that might meet them; 2) planning an actual classroom lesson (called a 'research lesson') that employs this strategy; 3) observing how the lesson works in practice; and 4) discussing and embedding revisions to enable improvement (Lewis, 2000). In addition, three pupils, who represent wider groups of interest, will be observed and their progress monitored as case studies of any impact of the approach (Dudley, 2011). In the Japanese model (referred to as *Jugyo Kenky*; Oyanagi, 2022) teachers also report on and often hold public demonstrations of the lesson, so that other teachers can benefit from their learning (Dudley, 2011, 2014); and it is noted by Lewis (2000) that Japanese teachers credit research lessons as the key to individual, school-wide and national improvements in teaching.

At the same time, the reasons for the success of JPD also serve as its main critique: specifically, that in trying to engage in JPD, busy and under-pressure teachers can often struggle with the demands of collaboration. Likewise, unless in trusting relationships, it can be off-putting for teachers knowing that their lessons and teaching will be observed and critiqued (e.g. see Tschannen-Moran, 2004; Gero, 2015). This therefore points to the vital role of school leaders in supporting PLNs – something we tackle below, and also in Chapter 6.

Trust

As we spotlight above and elsewhere, effective collaboration only occurs when there is **trust** between participants (Howland, 2015). Here, the notion of trust relates to our beliefs regarding the competence, benevolence and the integrity of another (Ehren, 2018). In particular, high levels of trust are associated with a variety of reciprocal efforts, including learning, complex information-sharing, joint problem-solving and shared decision-making. This is because, in high-trust situations, individuals feel supported and 'safe' to engage in risk-taking and the innovative behaviour associated with efforts at sharing, developing or trialling new practices (also Mintrop and Trujillo, 2007; Finnigan and Daly, 2012). In particular, a trusting work environment is instrumental in the type of 'double-loop' learning that is a prerequisite if teachers are to openly and collegiately challenge and question their foundational assumptions – as well as engage in ongoing and open disclosure about problems and challenges – as part of a process of seeking to continually improve teaching and learning (Argris and Schön, 1996). Trust takes time to develop (Greany and Wolfe, 2022), but can materialize more quickly when networking takes place between schools with similar quality features and similar context factors (Bremm and Drucks, 2018). This represents the notion of homogeneous networks, which contrasts with much of the perceived knowledge of self-improving school systems – such as in England – where networks can often comprise high- and low-achieving schools, in order that the latter can learn and benefit from engaging with the former (Chapman and Muijs, 2014; Howland, 2015; Muijs, 2015).

A commitment to reflective enquiry

The notion of reflective professional inquiry refers to the collaborative conversations teachers have about serious educational issues or problems. Research tells us that the collective generation and testing of ideas serves to enhance teachers' examination of their own practices (Stoll et al., 2006; Brown, 2020). As such, teachers should be actively and collectively questioning ineffective teaching routines, while finding proactive means to acknowledge and respond to them (Hubers and Poortman, 2018). Reaching a situation of being well informed means engaging with a range of perspectives through open debate and discussion (Stoll, 2010; Bauman, 2012); effective approaches to doing so include (Stoll et al., 2006):

1 'reflective dialogue': conversations about serious educational issues or problems involving the application of new knowledge in a sustained manner;
2 'deprivatization of practice': frequent examining of teachers' practice, through mutual observation and case analysis, joint planning and curriculum development (for instance, drawing on the Lesson Study approach above);
3 seeking new knowledge;
4 tacit knowledge constantly converted into shared knowledge through interaction; and
5 applying new ideas and information to problem-solving and solutions addressing pupils' needs.

Reflective professional inquiry is best achieved via meaningful 'learning conversations'. That is, situations in which there are: i) thoughtful (rather than superficial) discussion and challenge; ii) discussion and challenge focused on matters of teaching practice; and iii) attempts to consider evidence of actual and potential forms of practice. Obviously, i) to iii) should be undertaken with a view to developing both improved practice (i.e. new approaches to issues) and, as a result, improved outcomes for students.

What is vital here, is that learning conversations foster teachers' collective questioning with regard to issues such as the school's fundamental purpose or with regard to the implications of practices that have accumulated over time (Warren Little, 1990). Learning conversations result in the 'creation' of new knowledge (Brown, 2017, 2020), in the sense that multiple sets of knowledge are brought together to enable new understanding and the development of new practice.[1] To ensure knowledge creation is as effective as possible, high-quality learning conversations are likely to feature four characteristics (Stoll, 2012), as set out in Box 3.2.

---

1 As a direct result of studying successful Japanese businesses, Nonaka and Takeuchi (1995) proposed a four-stage model of knowledge creation comprising: socialization, externalization, combination and internalization. In this model, knowledge creation is considered to result from 'tapping [into] the tacit and often highly subjective insights, intuitions, and hunches of individual employees and making those insights available for testing and use by the company as a whole' (Nonaka, 1991: 97). Groups or individuals move through these four stages in a fixed order (Nonaka et al., 2008; Hubers, 2016): 1) in the socialization mode, tacit knowledge is shared, for example through describing one's own experiences, or observing experts; 2) in the externalization mode, the tacit knowledge of the socialization mode is made explicit through models, language, images and other forms of expression, and other external knowledge can be introduced; 3) in the combination mode, group members collect together explicit knowledge and define and edit it into a more complex and systematic set of knowledge; 4) in the internalization mode, group members critically reflect on the knowledge they created and put it into practice – here, knowledge becomes the foundation for new routines.

> **Box 3.2 The characteristics of high-quality learning conversations**
>
> The four key characteristics of high-quality learning conversations are:
>
> 1. **Focus on evidence and/or ideas.** Learning conversations are focused on two important perspectives. First, an understanding of existing and effective practice within the school. Second, ideas about innovation and transformation where, for example, the conversation explores creative ways to engage learners and extend learning. Both require all those participating in the learning conversation to be committed to the problem area in question, which in itself will need to be linked to the problem area being focused on within the PLN.
> 2. **Experience and external knowledge/theory.** Access to outside expertise deepens learning conversations. In the case of PLNs, such expertise will be held by participants as they return to their schools. Whether delivered personally, through writing or via other media, independent ideas are injected to stimulate reflection, challenge the status quo and extend thinking. Such ideas can help promote greater depth in conversations.
> 3. **Protocols and tools.** Learning conversations can often be framed more clearly when supported by frameworks and guidelines that help participants structure their dialogue and interrogate evidence or ideas. Teachers also need opportunities to look at and discuss 'artefacts' of their practice, not just test results.
> 4. **Facilitation.** Facilitation isn't the same as external expertise. It can come from inside or outside the group, but it is needed to elicit and support intellectual exchange, as well as maintaining open dialogue and, sometimes, injecting new energy into the conversation. Skilful facilitation can often lead to a productive balance of comfort and challenge. Further detail on facilitation is provided later in this chapter.

We have already outlined the importance of trust. In addition to facilitating collaboration, however, trust is also vital to developing reflective habits among teachers: that is, trust oils the process of teachers searching for new information and ideas in conjunction with others. The presence of trust also normalizes the notion of teachers experimenting with new ways of working (Kools and Stoll, 2016). This is because in high-trust situations, teachers feel supported to engage in the types of risk-taking and innovative behaviours associated with embracing change. In other words, they will more readily engage in efforts at developing or trialling new practices, since they perceive that it is 'safe' to do so. What's more, when individuals feel confident with one another in taking risks and feel able to expose vulnerabilities, they are generally better equipped to identify and voice problems, seek support and feedback, innovate and connect to others across the organization (Moolenaar and Sleegers, 2010). Interestingly, though, trust doesn't just materialize, and can quickly dissipate. This serves to spotlight the vital role of school leaders in securing levels of trust within schools.

The role of leadership in relation to PLNs

While it is most likely to be teachers that engage in networked learning activity, it is school leaders that need to support them in doing so, and thus the actions of school leaders are key to both maximizing the impact of PLNs and ensuring their longevity. School leaders have a substantive role in improving outcomes for children and young people (e.g. Marzano et al., 2005; Robinson et al., 2009). In fact, in terms of *within-school* factors, their impact is second only to that of teachers. School leaders can make a difference to teaching and learning through what are known as first- and second-order effects. To begin with, school leaders can target first-order variables. For instance, instructional leadership (see Box 3.3) can be used to improve the quality of teaching and the nature of the curriculum that is delivered to students in the classroom (Tulowitzki and Pietsch, 2018). School leaders are also able to generate second-order effects. Transformational leadership (see Box 3.3), for example, can be used to increase the commitment of others in the school in relation to specific first-order effects on learning (Tulowitzki and Pietsch, 2018). To get the most from engaging with PLNs, school leaders must therefore first understand their role as instructional leaders and the impact this role can have.

> **Box 3.3 Instructional and transformational school leadership**
>
> School leaders (that is, senior leaders such as headteachers or principals) are able to exert influence in their schools in a number of ways. As Day and Sammons (2013) note, such approaches include:
>
> 1. providing vision;
> 2. developing a common purpose, through consultation;
> 3. facilitating the achievement of organizational goals and fostering high performance expectations;
> 4. linking resource to outcomes;
> 5. working creatively and empowering others;
> 6. having a future orientation;
> 7. responding to diverse needs and situations;
> 8. supporting the school as a lively educational place;
> 9. ensuring that the curriculum and processes related to it are contemporary and relevant;
> 10. providing educational entrepreneurship.
>
> These approaches can be divided into the *transformational* aspects of leadership and *instructional* leadership.
>
> Transformational leadership is described as a process based on increasing the commitment of those in a school to organizational goals, vision and direction. Instructional leadership relates to the efforts of school leaders in improving teaching and learning in their school, as well as intentional improvements to the relationships between teachers, and the behaviour of teachers *vis-à-vis* their work with students.

Here, it is worth recalling the work of Robinson (e.g. Robinson et al., 2009; Robinson, 2011), where it is demonstrated that it is instructional leadership approaches which result in the most substantial benefits for student outcomes. In particular, Robinson et al. (2009) suggest that the act of school leadership with the biggest single impact for students is 'promoting and participating in teacher learning and development', which they indicate has an effect size of 0.84. This is double the effect size of the next highest impactful action: 'planning, coordinating and evaluating teaching and the curriculum' (ES 0.42), or indeed of the effect size of more transformational approaches. This link between student achievement and the active participation of school leaders in the professional learning and development of their staff leads Robinson et al. (2009: 201) to conclude that: '[the] more leaders focus their relationships, their work and their learning on the core business of teaching and learning the greater their influence on student outcomes'. This means that a school leader's main focus and responsibility should be promoting better outcomes for students, emphasizing the importance of teaching and learning, and enhancing teacher quality (Day and Sammons, 2013). Likewise, in creating and fostering an organizational culture of collaboration rather than competition, school leaders can positively impact on the trusting relationships and trustworthy behaviour of teachers, meaning they will work together more effectively to learn and develop (Tschannen-Moran and Hoy, 2000). Correspondingly, transformational aspects of leadership, such as establishing goals and expectations (which Robinson et al. (2009) suggest has an effect size of 0.35), or providing the necessary resource and structures (e.g. time and space to support a given way of working – ES 0.34), should thus be employed in pursuit of specific instructional goals or the introduction of new ones (Leithwood et al., 2006).

As well as having an instructional focus, as we note in Chapter 1, school leaders must also lead ethically, with a commitment to social justice and doing the best for each child. But an ethical instructional approach is only one requirement for schools to engage effectively with PLNs. This is because school leaders must actively want to network with others in the first place. In other words, they must possess an inherent desire to reach out beyond the boundaries of their school and wish for their teachers to engage in collaborative endeavours with others (Armstrong et al., 2021). As Azorín (2018: presentation slides) notes, 'the schools we want today are not institutions that sit behind their railings, but rather organisations that are prepared to boldly open up and work in collaborative networks with their neighbours and other allies'. This is not always an easy task, when schools are facing demands of ever higher levels of achievement coupled with an intolerance of failure (Muijs et al., 2010); this often means the natural inclination of school leaders is to focus inwards and to 'put one's own house in order' first. Nonetheless, effective engagement with PLNs requires school leaders to adopt an external focus and to couple their desire to do the best for their students and their understanding of their role as instructional leaders, with a recognition that instructional ethical leadership can often best be served through collaborative work. Coupling an external focus with their moral driver for their students results in school leaders needing to:

- Sign up to the common purposes of the network and the focus area of networked activity (Muijs, 2015; Sartory et al., 2017). As we discussed in Chapter 1, a shared sense of purpose among the individual PLN members in relation to the specific goals of the PLN is key. Although members do not have to have homogeneous goals for participating in the PLN (as goals can vary due to individual learning goals, vision on education and so forth), the more these goals are aligned and PLN members agree on the reasons why they are working in this group, the easier it will be to meet everyone's expectations.
- Understand that change through networks requires time to come to fruition. Time is a scarce commodity and scarcer still in education systems now dominated by short-term rather than long-term success. As Bauman (2012) notes, these days practitioners are more often than not looking at the next few moves ahead rather than progress towards a long-term attainable goal, especially if they perceive they will not be in post in the longer term (Robinson et al., 2009).
- Recognize that, to ensure the successful ongoing operation of the network, common resources might need to be established (e.g. new resource generated or existing resources transferred) and that these resources will need to be maintained over the mid to long term (Gilbert, 2017; Sartory et al., 2017). At the same time, any transfer of committed resource must not impact negatively on the internal functioning of the schools involved.
- Acknowledge a moral obligation towards, and an acceptance of collective responsibility for, the outcomes of all children in all schools in the network (Gilbert, 2017). In other words, schools engage in networks to gain in terms of their teachers' learning but should also be supporting teachers in other schools with their own learning requirements. PLN activity can also, of course, represent an extension of a school leader's moral purpose, enabling them to carry their values and vision beyond the school gates.
- Recognize that distributed leadership needs to be supported if it is to flourish, since network leaders and participants will not necessarily also be formal leaders (Dimmock, 2019, with more detail on distributed leadership in Chapter 5; as argued by Díaz-Gibson et al. (2017: 1044), 'networked leadership is considered to be a different type of nonhierarchical leadership'. This means that PLN participants are supported to engage in networked activity and to lead change in their own school. This represents a stark contrast to many schools, where the impetus for change and the introduction of new ideas often comes from the school leader themselves (Finnigan et al., 2013).

Once prepared to engage in networked forms of learning, to ensure it leads to positive impacts for their schools, school leaders must also actively work at making the PLN activity a success. This means supporting teachers to achieve a lasting change in their practice as well as measurably positive student outcomes (Hubers and Poortman, 2018). Furthermore, success means that all educators with links to the network in question should display 'agency': in other words, leaders actively support the ongoing and active process of practice innovation. To make it easy to remember, the actions required by school leaders to do so can be corralled under the three headings of prioritization, formalization and mobilization (Brown and Flood, 2019); detail on each of these is provided in Chapter 2.

Who will run the PLN?

The final thing to consider in this chapter is who will actually organize and facilitate the PLN. Magic as they are, PLNs don't run themselves, and for the PLN approach to be as effective as possible you will need to recruit someone responsible for (among other things):

1 organizing PLN activity to ensure meetings are held, activity resourced and facilitated, etc.;
2 supporting the effective dynamics/interpersonal relationships between PLN participants – for instance, facilitators will need to ensure that a trusting environment is actively fostered, so that meaningful inter-school collaborative activity occurs;
3 ensuring the PLN can be sustained long enough for its work to be completed;
4 ensuring that PLN activity leads to the learning/gaining of new knowledge by participants;
5 helping to build capacity for PLN participants to engage, both in PLN activity and in terms of linking this activity to their school;
6 effectively influencing at the school leadership level to ensure there is effective support and engagement in PLN activity, etc.

How you find and resource a facilitator will, of course, also depend on governance arrangements for your PLN. This is because, typically, networks tend to be either formal and contracted in nature or informal and voluntary (Ehren and Godfrey, 2017; Armstrong et al., 2021). Formal, contracted networks are invariably goal-directed and benefit from more stable patterns of social relations, deliberate interactions and structure in the shape of organizational arrangements and rules. There is little evidence to suggest, however, that either formal or informal networks have more or less impact on teaching and learning outcomes. At the same time, formal networks are likely to involve the intentional commitment of resources, meaning a facilitator can often be funded to support the PLN on a full- or part-time basis (e.g. see Chapman and Muijs, 2014). In a similar vein, the leadership and governance of networks can vary from non-brokered shared governance to being highly brokered by one organization, and from participant-led to externally led (Ehren and Godfrey, 2017). Here, highly brokered governance tends to be more effective when networks are larger. This is because trust, as well as consensus regarding the purpose of the network, tends to decrease as a function of size, while the time, effort and skill required to coordinate the network increases (Ehren and Godfrey, 2017). Shared governance, on the other hand, is most likely to be effective when trust is pervasive throughout the network and the more homogeneous nature of smaller networks provides a strong basis for bottom-up collaboration among network participants (Ehren and Godfrey, 2017). Correspondingly, the choice of who takes charge of PLN administration and organization depends not only on the size of your PLN now, but also on where you see it heading in the future.

> **Chapter take-aways**
> - PLNs should only be considered truly successful when they lead to lasting school-wide changes in teaching practices, and these changes result in measurably positive outcomes. What's more, all educators with links to a network should also display 'agency'. This means that teachers in schools engaged in PLN activity should be actively trying to innovate their practices in an ongoing way.
> - For PLNs to endure and be successful, a number of conditions need to be in place. These include: a shared sense of purpose, centred on student learning; a spirit of trust and mutual dependence; a commitment to reflective inquiry and effective leadership. Also needed is meaningful enquiry, or *joint work*, with digital technologies increasingly changing the ways in which joint work can materialize.
> - On a practical level, networks also need effective facilitation. How you find and resource a facilitator depends on the exact governance arrangements for your PLN. In all cases, however, network facilitators will need a range of skills if the PLN is to function effectively. These skills have been nicely summarized by Greany and Wolfe (2022) as relating to facilitators' ability to convene PLNs, catalyse PLN activity and to coach both participants and those school leaders with links to the PLN.

References

Argris, C. and Schön, D. (1996) *Organisational Learning II: Theory, Method, Practice, Increasing Professional Effectiveness*. San Francisco, CA: Jossey-Bass.

Armstrong, P. and Brown, C. (2022) *School to School Collaboration: Learning Across International Contexts*. London: Emerald.

Armstrong, P., Brown, C. and Chapman, C. (2021) School to school collaboration in England: A configurative review of the empirical evidence, *Review of Education*, 9(1): 319–51.

Azorín, C. (2018) Networking in education: Lessons from Southampton. Presented at the European Conference on Educational Research annual meeting, Bolzano (Italy), 4–7 September.

Bauman, Z. (2012) *Liquid Modernity*. Cambridge: Polity Press.

Bremm, N. and Drucks, S. (2018) Building up school to school networks using an evidence-based approach. Presented at the European Conference on Educational Research annual meeting, Bolzano (Italy), 4–7 September.

Brown, C. (2017) Research Learning Communities: How the RLC approach enables teachers to use research to improve their practice and the benefits for students that occur as a result, *Research for All*, 1(2): 387–405.

Brown, C. (2020) *The Networked School Leader: How to Improve Teaching and Student Outcomes using Learning Networks*. Bingley: Emerald.

Brown, C. and Flood, J. (2019) *Formalise, Prioritise and Mobilise: How School Leaders Secure the Benefits of Professional Learning Networks*. London: Emerald.

Cameron, A. and Farrar, M. (2022) Change, adaptation and transformation: Peer review and collaborative improvement during the time of Covid, in G. Handscomb and C. Brown (eds) *The Power of Professional Learning Networks: Traversing the Present; Transforming the Future*. Woodbridge: John Catt, pp. 59–74.

Chapman, C. and Muijs, D. (2014) Does school-to-school collaboration promote school improvement? A study of the impact of school federations on student outcomes, *School Effectiveness and School Improvement*, 25(3): 351–93.

Cheung, W.M. and Wong, W.Y. (2014) Does Lesson Study work? A systematic review on the effects of Lesson Study and learning study on teachers and students, *International Journal for Lesson and Learning Studies*, 3(2): 137–49.

Day, C. and Sammons, P. (2013) *Successful Leadership: A Review of the International Literature*. Reading: CfBT Education Trust.

Díaz-Gibson, J., Zaragoza, M.C., Daly, A.J., Mayayo, M.J. and Romaní, J.R. (2017) Networked leadership in Educational Collaborative Networks, *Educational Management Administration & Leadership*, 45(6): 1040–59.

Dimmock, C. (2019) Leading research-informed practice in schools, in D. Godfrey and C. Brown (eds) *An Eco-System for Research Engaged Schools: Reforming Education through Research*. London: Sage, pp. 56–72.

Dudley, P. (2011) Lesson Study development in England: From school networks to national policy, *International Journal for Lesson and Learning Studies*, 1(1): 85–100.

Dudley, P. (2014) *Lesson Study: A Handbook*. Available at http://lessonstudy.co.uk/wp-content/uploads/2014/01/new-handbook-early-years-edition2014-version.pdf (accessed 15 February 2022).

Ehren, M. (2018) Accountability and trust: two sides of the same coin? Invited talk as part of the University of Oxford's Intelligent Accountability Symposium II, Oxford, 12 December.

Ehren, M. and Godfrey, D. (2017) External accountability of collaborative arrangements: A case study of a Multi Academy Trust in England, *Education Assessment Evaluation and Accountability*, 29: 339–62.

Fielding, M., Bragg, S., Craig, J. et al. (2005) Factors influencing the transfer of good practice. Available at http://webarchive.nationalarchives.gov.uk/20130401151715/http://www.education.gov.uk/publications/eOrderingDownload/RR615.pdf.pdf (accessed 15 February 2022).

Finnigan, K. and Daly, A. (2012) Mind the gap: Organizational learning and improvement in an underperforming urban system, *American Journal of Education*, 119(1): 41–71.

Finnigan, K., Daly, A. and Che, J. (2013) Systemwide reform in districts under pressure: The role of social networks in defining, acquiring, using, and diffusing research evidence, *Journal of Educational Administration*, 51(4): 476–97.

Fraser, P. and Fulop, G. (2022) Fostering school collaboration across schools around the world: Insights from TALIS, in G. Handscomb and C. Brown (eds) *The Power of Professional Learning Networks: Traversing the Present; Transforming the Future*. Woodbridge, John Catt, pp. 43–58.

Gero, G. (2015) The prospects of Lesson Study in the US: Teacher support and comfort within a district culture of control, *International Journal for Lesson and Learning Studies*, 4(1): 7–25.

Gilbert, C. (2017) *Optimism of the Will: The Development of Local Area-Based Education Partnerships. A Think Piece*. London: London Centre for Leadership in Learning.

Greany, T. and Wolfe, A. (2022) Networking small rural schools in the pandemic, in G. Handscomb and C. Brown (eds) *The Power of Professional Learning Networks: Traversing the Present; Transforming the Future*. Woodbridge, John Catt, pp. 75–90.

Howland, G. (2015) Structural reform: The experience of ten schools driving the development of an all-age hard federation across a market town in northern England, *Management in Education*, 29(1): 25–30.

Hubers, M. and Poortman, C. (2018) Establishing sustainable school improvement through Professional Learning Networks, in C. Brown and C. Poortman (eds) *Networks for Learning: Effective Collaboration for Teacher, School and System Improvement*. London: Routledge, pp. 194–204.

Kools, M. and Stoll, L. (2016) *What Makes a School a Learning Organisation?*, OECD Education Working Papers, No. 137. Paris: OECD Publishing. Available at https://doi.org/10.1787/5jlwm62b3bvh-en.

Leithwood, K., Day, C., Sammons, P., Harris, A. and Hopkins, D. (2006) *Successful School Leadership: What it is and How it Influences Student Learning*, Research Report 800. London: DfES.

Lewis, C. (2000) Lesson Study: The core of Japanese professional development. Paper presented at the Annual Meeting of the American Educational Research Association, New Orleans, LA, 24–28 April.

Marzano, J., Waters, T. and McNulty, B. (2005) *School Leadership that Works: From Research to Results*. Alexandria, VA: ASCD.

Mintrop, H. and Trujillo, T. (2007) The practical relevance of accountability systems for school improvement: A descriptive analysis of California schools, *Educational Evaluation and Policy Analysis*, 29(4): 319–52.

Moolenaar, N. and Sleegers, P. (2010) Social networks, trust, and innovation: The role of relationships in supporting an innovative climate in Dutch schools, in A. Daly (ed.) *Social Network Theory and Educational Change*. Cambridge, MA: Harvard Education Press, pp. 97–114.

Muijs, D. (2015) Improving schools through collaboration: A mixed methods study of school-to-school partnerships in the primary sector, *Oxford Review of Education*, 41(5): 563–86.

Muijs, D., West, M. and Ainscow, M. (2010) Why network? Theoretical perspectives on networking, *School Effectiveness and School Improvement*, 21(1): 5–26.

Oyanagi, W. (2022) Influence of evidence-informed practice on teachers' professional identity and leadership in Japan, in C. Brown and J. Malin (eds) *The Handbook of Evidence-Informed Practice in Education: Learning from International Contexts*. London: Emerald, pp. 353–64.

Rempe-Gillen, E. (2018) Primary school teacher experiences in cross-phase professional development collaborations, *Professional Development in Education*, 44(3): 356–68.

Robinson, V. (2011) *Student Centred Leadership*. San Francisco, CA: Jossey-Bass.

Robinson, V., Hohepa, M. and Lloyd, D. (2009) *School Leadership and Student Outcomes: Identifying What Works and Why: Best Evidence Synthesis*. Wellington, NZ: Ministry of Education.

Sartory, K., Jungermann, A. and Järvinen, H. (2017) Support for school-to-school networks: How networking teachers perceive external support by a local coordinating agency, *British Journal of Educational Studies*, 65(2): 143–65.

Sebba, J., Tregenza, J. and Kent, P. (2012) *Powerful Professional Learning: A School Leader's Guide to Joint Practice Development*. Nottingham: National College for School Leadership.

Stoll, L. (2010) Connecting learning communities: Capacity building for systemic change, in A. Hargreaves, A. Lieberman, M. Fullan and D. Hopkins (eds) *Second International Handbook of Educational Change*. Dordrecht: Springer, pp. 469–84.

Stoll, L. (2012) Stimulating learning conversations, *Professional Development Today*, 14(4): 6–12.

Stoll, L., Bolam, R., McMahon, A., Wallace, M. and Thomas, S. (2006) Professional learning communities: A review of the literature, *Journal of Educational Change*, 7(4): 221–58.

Tschannen-Moran, M. (2004) *Trust Matters: Leadership for Successful Schools*. San Francisco, CA: Jossey-Bass.

Tschannen-Moran, M. and Hoy, W.K. (2000) A multidisciplinary analysis of the nature, meaning, and measurement of trust, *Review of Educational Research*, 70(4): 547–93.

Tulowitzki, P. and Pietsch, M. (2018) The differential and shared effects of leadership for learning on teachers' organizational commitment and job satisfaction: A multilevel analysis. Presented at the European Conference on Educational Research annual meeting, Bolzano (Italy), 4–7 September.

Warren Little, J. (1990) The persistence of privacy: Autonomy and initiative in teachers' professional relations, *Teachers College Record*, 91(4): 509–35.

4 Trials and rewards – adopting cycles of inquiry

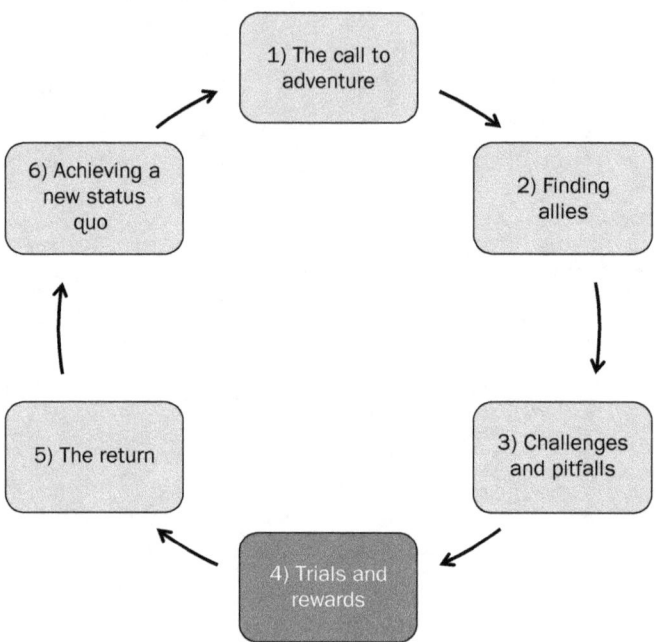

One of the main factors that will determine whether your PLN is successful is a commitment to reflective inquiry. Engaging in a PLN can lead to improved outcomes for students, but only if educators do something different from before. And for this difference to occur, teacher learning is often required. That is what 'reflective professional inquiry' (RPI) is all about (Brown et al., 2021). In this chapter, we discuss several ways of engaging in reflective inquiry (via what is known as cycles of inquiry) before settling on the key steps that readers will need to take. Other practical tools that are vital to this type of approach – such as lesson planning/observation – are also outlined, ensuring readers can run networked learning sessions and the process as a whole effectively.

What makes a conversation reflective?

Teachers and school leaders have a lot of meetings occurring at a variety of different levels in their schools. Think about a typical week – there will be regular team meetings, department meetings, teacher–parent meetings, professional development days, and the like. Consider some of the meetings that you had recently with two or more colleagues: how effective were these meetings? What were they about, and what made them go well or not so well? Much of the conversation that occurs in schools is centred on administrative topics, things that went well or did not go well in the recent week, but do not really concern outcomes for students or ways to improve such outcomes (we have also seen instances where a lot of the meeting held is given over to thinking about dates and planning for future meetings!; Zala-Mezö and Egli, 2022).

Teachers participating in PLNs often really value exchanging experiences and anecdotes about their practice. This is important and serves the purpose of getting to know each other and developing trust and inspiration. This type of exchange is not usually enough, however, to achieve the kind of learning necessary to realize positive change for students. Moreover, the focus of a meeting can often be on directly *doing* rather than *investigating* issues first: in other words, addressing the symptoms rather than the cause. As a result, challenges, problems and ideas are invariably responded to with short-term action, rather than questions about what is going on and why. Of course, we want issues to be solved as soon as possible after we have noticed them. At the same time, it is much more likely that we will *actually* solve them if we know what is happening, what is causing the current situation, and what research tells us about how the problem has been solved elsewhere. Thus, by taking action immediately, we run the risk of spending valuable resources on something that does not work at all, and it usually takes a while before this becomes apparent. Consequently, if we are trying to address problems or innovation goals to improve outcomes for students, which are often not very basic in nature, a more elaborate process of collaborative learning is needed (typically one that fosters cognitive dissonance – see Box 4.1 for more here).

Box 4.1 Fostering cognitive dissonance

There are a number of ways individuals can change their beliefs (theories) in the presence of new evidence. For instance, when faced with anomalous data that challenge currently held theories, individuals may find themselves ignoring, rejecting or excluding it from the theory domain, holding it in abeyance (to perhaps be dealt with at a later time), reinterpreting it to fit the theory, modifying the theory slightly to accommodate the data, or the data can be accepted and the theory changed. It is only this last reaction – which involves the creation of cognitive dissonance – however, that will lead to a substantive change in beliefs (Chinn and Brewer, 1993).

In the literature, many different terms are used to refer essentially to this same concept of reflective professional inquiry, for instance: deep-level collaboration, reflective dialogue, learning conversations, depth of inquiry, and generative discourse (Schildkamp et al., 2016; Vangrieken et al., 2017; Brown, 2018; Zala-Mezö and Egli, 2022). Researchers have developed a range of guidelines and protocols to structure such forms of reflective professional inquiry, so as to ensure it can actually *help teachers make sense of various forms of evidence to drive real changes in student learning* (Earl and Timperley, 2008: 2; Brown, 2018: 40; see also Schildkamp et al., 2016 and Box 2.1). We have provided a few examples of these in Box 4.2.

Box 4.2 Supporting reflective conversations

RLNs: As we note in Chapter 1, The RLN model involves participants attending four workshops over the course of an academic year (October to June), with the content of these workshops as follows:

- **Workshop one:** participants focus on understanding the research and current practitioner-held knowledge about the specific issues being explored (for example, how to ensure children develop growth mindsets).
- **Workshop two:** participants explore the baseline in more detail, develop a research-informed approach to improving practice within each school and consider how this approach might be trialled effectively.
- **Workshop three:** participants are enabled to refine their approaches; this workshop is also used to introduce the idea of whole school change as well as change tools and change approaches.
- **Workshop four:** participants consider both the impact their work has achieved and how to share knowledge of impact more widely.

As part of this process, a specific learning conversation approach utilizes protocols and exercises to help participants engage in conversations focused on bringing together research knowledge with participants' own experience and knowledge about their teaching context (for example, in terms of 'improving maths outcomes for looked after children', e.g. those recently in social care). One such protocol for helping educators consider how academic research links to their own understanding is presented below (see Chapter 1 for further details).

Research theme connection to knowledge and practice

... connects with our own knowledge and practice	... deepens our knowledge and practice	... challenges our knowledge and practice

On completion, this knowledge is then used as the basis for further action.

Lesson Study: Lesson Study is widely used in Japan as professional development practice (Cheung and Wong, 2014). As a process, Lesson Study involves teachers collaborating, normally in groups of three, to progress cycles of iterative practice development. Such cycles typically involve the following steps: 1) a discussion of student learning goals and the identification of a teaching strategy that might meet them; 2) planning an actual classroom lesson (called a 'research lesson') that employs this strategy; 3) observing how the lesson works in practice; and 4) discussing and embedding revisions to enable improvement (Lewis, 2000). In addition, three pupils, who represent wider groups of interest, will be observed and their progress monitored as case studies of the impact of the approach (Dudley, 2011).

Data teams: Schildkamp et al. (2016: 232) use a number of steps to structure data team conversations so as to foster teachers engaging in 'deep' forms of enquiry (see Schildkamp et al., 2018 and Box 2.1). In the first step of problem definition, for example, participants need to gather and analyse data to establish the extent of the problem and the desired goal. Next comes developing hypotheses regarding the cause of the problem. Here, participants brainstorm and categorize a range of possible causes (also drawing on input from colleagues outside of the data team). Participants follow specific sub-steps for data analysis and drawing conclusions (main steps 3–6), and make use of templates (and literature) to develop and plan for taking actions to solve the problem (step 7). In the eighth and final step, data are again collected about whether the problem has been reduced or the goal has been achieved, but also about the implementation process of the actions.

The examples in Box 4.2 show that quite a lot of main steps, sub-steps, protocols and templates can be used to support reflective inquiry-based conversations in meetings. Simultaneously, the RLN and data team examples show that such learning conversations also need to involve those outside of the PLN, as well as to take place in between PLN engagements (for instance, because data and/or literature will need to be gathered in between meetings or be discussed more widely with colleagues in one's 'home school'). Moreover, reflecting on evidence, discussing it with colleagues outside the PLN – and also using their input – as well as applying their insights when evaluating the effects of your new intervention, are all essential elements in this process. There are many other examples of approaches in addition to those we outline above (for instance, Teacher Design Teams (Binkhorst, 2018) or Spirals of Inquiry (Kaser and Halbert, 2017)). So, what have we learned from these approaches and activities that helps support the process of a PLN's reflective professional inquiry? We'll now explore this in more detail.

The reflective professional inquiry process

Reflective professional inquiry (RPI) in PLNs is a process in which teachers collaboratively learn, and innovate their teaching practice, in relation to pressing educational problems or goals they would like to achieve. They do this by generating and testing ideas based on literature and/or data both within and also in between PLN meetings over a period of time. The literature (e.g. Schildkamp et al., 2016; Kaser and Halbert, 2017; Binkhorst, 2018; Brown et al., 2021; Wigman, 2022) shows that RPI can be understood as a process with four main components:

1 PLNs need to start by *formulating a collaborative goal for improvement in terms of outcomes for students* (we covered this in Chapter 1):

   - Current success(es) and/or challenge(s) are the starting point for developing this goal.
   - These successes and/or challenges are derived based on data of the current situation in teachers' own practice.
   - Formulating a goal guiding the PLN is not a one-moment-one-meeting type of activity. It starts with a theme that is considered challenging, e.g. 'motivational problems', 'poor mathematics results', 'inequity'. Assumptions, feelings, prejudice and other types of ideas that have not yet been confirmed about the theme usually play a role in determining the need for a PLN. Once it has been decided to start, based on data confirming the need for change, it is important to formulate a much more focused, clear and even measurable goal to guide further PLN activities and evaluate their success at the end of the process.

2 The second step is about *developing an idea to achieve the goal* by investigating, based on data and/or research evidence from professional and scientific literature (we also covered this in Chapter 1):

- Cause(s) of problems in current outcomes for students, as well as the factors that can help lead to the achievement of the goal.
- What needs to be learned to achieve the goal, not only by students, but first by teachers to change their practice.

3 Third, *taking action to solve causes of problems* and/or positively influence factors that help achieve the goal is key:

- This includes thinking about who is involved and how to secure their engagement.
- Considering what activities and resources needed to be implemented when.

4 Fourth, to complete the cycle of inquiry, *evaluating the process and outcomes, and reflection* is vital to determine:

- Were the actions implemented as intended? How were they experienced by students and teachers?
- What have we learned as a network and as individual members?
- How effective were the actions: has the goal, in terms of outcomes for students, been achieved?
- Do the actions or the goal need to be adapted? If the goal has not yet been achieved, for instance, implementation of actions might need to be adjusted. If the goals have been achieved sooner than expected, should a more ambitious goal have been set?

In relation to this fourth and final stage, it is clear that what underpins any approach to evaluation is being able to measure change. Understanding what to measure is not always easy, however. In Box 4.3 we provide a way of thinking about what to measure and how, if we are to understand changes in our understanding and that of our colleagues, changes in teacher behaviours, changes in student outcomes, and also whether policies, procedures or approaches to communication need changing to support the implementation of what we are proposing. Of course when considering such approaches it is always good to keep in mind the following questions: i) how easy will it be to collect data at these different levels?; ii) over what timescales does such data need to be measured?; iii) how confident are we in being able to design research tools/instruments to gather this type of data?; and iv) what mechanisms do we have in place to act on the data?

Box 4.3 Understanding impact (from Guskey, 2000)

Level of evaluation	How information will be gathered	What is measured or assessed	How information can be used
1 Participant's reaction	Questionnaires administered at the end of a session	Initial response to and satisfaction with the 'experience'	To improve initial communication of the idea as well as its design
2 Participant's learning	Demonstrations Participant reflections Participant portfolios	New knowledge and skills of participants	To improve programme content, format, organization
3 Organization support and change	Questionnaires Interviews School records Participant portfolios	The organization's advocacy, support, accommodation, facilitation and recognition	To document and improve organizational support To inform future change efforts
4 Participant's use of new knowledge and skills	Questionnaires Structured interviews Participant reflection Participant portfolios Direct observation	Degree and quality of implementation	To document and improve the implementation of programme content
5 Student learning outcomes	Student records School records Questionnaires Structured interviews Participant portfolios	Student learning outcomes: cognitive, affective, psychomotor	To focus and improve all aspects of programme design, implementation and follow-up To demonstrate overall impact of professional development

The wider environment of the school in question

But when it comes to RPI there will be other factors that we will also want to consider, since they interact with and influence each of the four components above. For instance, we need to think about the extent to which a trusting environment exists within the school in question, whether there is currently a culture of innovation in the school and whether there are any cultural norms regarding the specific type of innovation to be introduced. Regarding the first of these, many of the concepts that have been discussed above cannot function without the existence of a high-trust environment. For instance, for learning conversations to function effectively, educators need to feel able to expose gaps in their knowledge as well as experiment with what emerges from such conversations (Brown, 2018). Likewise, forms of Joint Practice Development (e.g. the Lesson Study approach featured in Box 4.2) can be off-putting for teachers, who may be uncomfortable that their lessons and teaching will be observed and critiqued, unless this activity is undertaken in a situation where trust is high (e.g. see Tschannen-Moran, 2004).

Trust is also vital more generally to how effective social networks in schools share and adopt innovation (Warren Little, 1990; Mitton et al., 2007; Sebba et al., 2012). For instance, it is argued by Finnigan and Daly (2012) that where educators feel they do not have the knowledge or skills to challenge the introduction of an innovation, trust enables a given innovation to be widely adopted. In other words, trust helps signify that it is safe or okay to use this innovation. What's more, higher levels of trust are significantly associated with more frequent (and useful) relationships between individuals, which benefits a variety of relationship-related efforts, including collaboration, learning, complex information-sharing and problem-solving, shared decision-making, and coordinated action: i.e. the actions essential to the take-up and use of innovations emerging from PLNs, or the subsequent development of these in Professional Learning Communities (PLCs) (Tschannen-Moran, 2004; Bryk et al., 2010). The notion of trust also flags once again the importance of having the 'right people in the room': ensuring PLN members and their allies are those who are trusted, and so well connected within their intra-school networks – which means they are likely to ensure change happens in schools. As a result, the notion of trust can also be explicitly linked to what we understand about effective social networks and who might be most central within them (Brown, 2018).

A second key factor to consider is the existence of any historical norms regarding innovation and adoption generally (Rogers, 1995). As Warren Little (1990: 530) notes, the likelihood of new innovations being able to influence individuals rests, in part, on their congruence with established behaviours regarding the adoption of 'the new'. Schools particularly attuned to innovation are sometimes referred to as *learning organizations* (LOs). The OECD publication *What Makes a School a Learning Organisation?* (Kools and Stoll, 2016) suggests schools operating as LOs are viewed as having a dynamic, adaptive culture for change, within which a range of strategies can be accessed to address the needs of the particular school community and, ultimately, the learning needs of all students. In keeping with the section above, LOs also place an emphasis on the development of professional relationships, which build a school climate of trust and cooperation (Silins and Mulford, 2004). It is likely to be easy to broker innovations within innovative school cultures or within LOs. If such a culture does not currently exist, however, this can be promoted by school leaders. For instance, school leaders may extol the benefits of considering innovative ideas and normalizing the notion of experimenting with new ways of working (Leithwood et al., 2006) (see Chapter 3 for more here) – not least by modelling an 'inquiry habit of mind': i.e. senior leaders actively and visibly seeking out a range of perspectives to help them address given issues; purposefully seeking relevant information from numerous and diverse sources; and continually exploring new ways to tackle perennial problems. Likewise, the assumptions underpinning proposed new practices need to be made explicit by school leaders in order that they can be challenged and improved (Halbert et al., 2011; Schildkamp and Ehren, 2012). School leaders also need to ensure that an environment exists which enables new practices to be trialled, evaluated and refined (Datnow et al., 2013). School leaders should therefore put in place structures so that knowledge can be shared. This includes making available and coordinating time (and related processes) to enable teachers to discuss new approaches to practice.

Third, consideration needs to be given to the cultural norms regarding the specific type of innovation: for instance, whether 'formative assessment' is currently standard teaching practice (Rogers, 1995). If the innovative practice is totally distinct from what has been done previously, evidence suggests that a number of factors can be influential in its adoption, including the context of the school, as well as wider pressures and forces shaping the environment in which given schools are situated; the resources available to the school; the capacity and capability of the staff in the school; practical aspects of implementation, such as existing routines; and current norms within the school (Koutsouris and Norwich, 2018; Neal et al., 2019).

And now the irrational

But while much of the above may seem commonsensical, what about other aspects that might be less immediately apparent but will still affect RPI? Such as, for instance, the role of emotion. The field of art and design provides a useful insight into how emotion might be used to facilitate (or indeed hinder) RPI. Take the work of leading design academic Donald Norman, for instance, who argues that 'the emotional system is a powerful information processing system that determines whether a situation is safe or threatening, whether something that is happening is good or bad, desirable or not' (2013: 47). In tense and threatening situations, the emotional system will trigger the release of hormones that bias the brain in preparation for action. In calm, non-threatening situations, the emotional system triggers the release of hormones that bias the brain towards exploration and creativity (Norman, 2013). A positive emotional state is therefore ideal for reflective thought, while a brain in a negative emotional state provides focus: precisely what is needed to maintain attention on a task and finish it.

This links nicely with the educational perspectives provided by Schildkamp and Datnow (2020: 18), who argue that how practitioners view the purpose of the PLN is vital. PLN efforts focused on accountability are far less fruitful than those focused on continuous improvement, or with an explicit focus on equity, which are far more likely to lead to educational policies and practices that expand students' opportunities to learn. Schildkamp and Datnow (2020) also link such outcomes to emotion and suggest that when teachers have negative experiences with data use, such as shaming and blaming, or feel that their time is being wasted, they are far less likely to be engaged. Positive experiences, on the other hand (for example, working with a productive team that is delving deeply into learning), are likely to encourage teachers to become more engaged and in turn more reflective (display higher levels of depth of inquiry).

Cycles of inquiry

The RPI process is, accordingly, not only about finding 'the' right solution as soon as possible (Schildkamp and Poortman, 2022), but also about learning together how educational problems and ambitions can be realized in an evidence-informed (i.e. based on data and literature) but also contextually meaningful way. If this is achieved, the network and its participants are enabled to also address new issues meaningfully. To achieve sustainable school improvement (see also Chapter 6), this process never stops, and new cycles of inquiry are engaged in for new problems and ambitions. Thus, while the four RPI steps described above might reflect quite a straightforward approach, in reality the RPI process is not neatly defined, or linear, and will be constantly buffeted by environmental factors as people come and go and contexts evolve. This is a complex process in which you may go back and forth between steps to fine-tune, especially where new insights might require adaptations of the goal, ideas and actions that everyone had previously agreed on. Coming together regularly for a sufficient amount of time is essential to enable an intensive learning process. Many variants are possible, for instance the four-workshop approach used by RLNs, with four one-hour workshops spread over a period of a year (or even eight two-hour workshops if time is tight), or the data team approach with meetings every three to four weeks over a school year period (Schildkamp et al., 2019): whatever works to fit the context of the PLN. Without wishing to prescribe such formats exactly, research tells us that longer-term professional development with a larger number of hours (Yoon et al., 2007; Van Veen et al., 2010) works better than short-term and less intensive approaches.

We also know, with our post-Covid hats on, that technology can now help ameliorate some of the time-related issues that occur when PLNs are not geographically close (for instance, schools in rural areas). Here the effective use of digital and social media can save hours of travel time but still lead to effective collaboration. Examples of successful digitally led PLNs include:

- **The Scottish Islands School Network:** a network of leadership teams working in schools across the rural Scottish isles (Dick and Peat, 2022). A predominantly online entity, the network now forms a flourishing 'space' in which participants are able to share professional knowledge, experiences and resources between those in a similar context, and enable schools to expand the educational programmes they offer, as well as put in place specialized support and extracurricular activities for students.
- **Church of England Foundation for Educational Leadership:** launched in 2019 with the aim of supporting senior leaders in small rural schools in England, these digitally facilitated PLNs focus on the sharing of resources, ideas and practice in relation to faith leadership and social action, as well as building relationships with other school leaders. Their online and faith-based presence also meant these PLNs served an additional function during the Covid-19 lockdown, however: that of helping participating leaders to sustain themselves and to refill their 'reservoirs of hope' during difficult and challenging times (Greany and Wolfe, 2022).

Successfully collaborating and learning together in the PLN also depends on successfully sharing and further developing the knowledge built up within the PLN with other colleagues in participants' 'home schools' (see Chapter 3 and Poortman and Brown, 2021). PLN participant colleagues also need to incorporate

Box 4.4 Visualizing the process of reflective professional inquiry/ cycles of inquiry

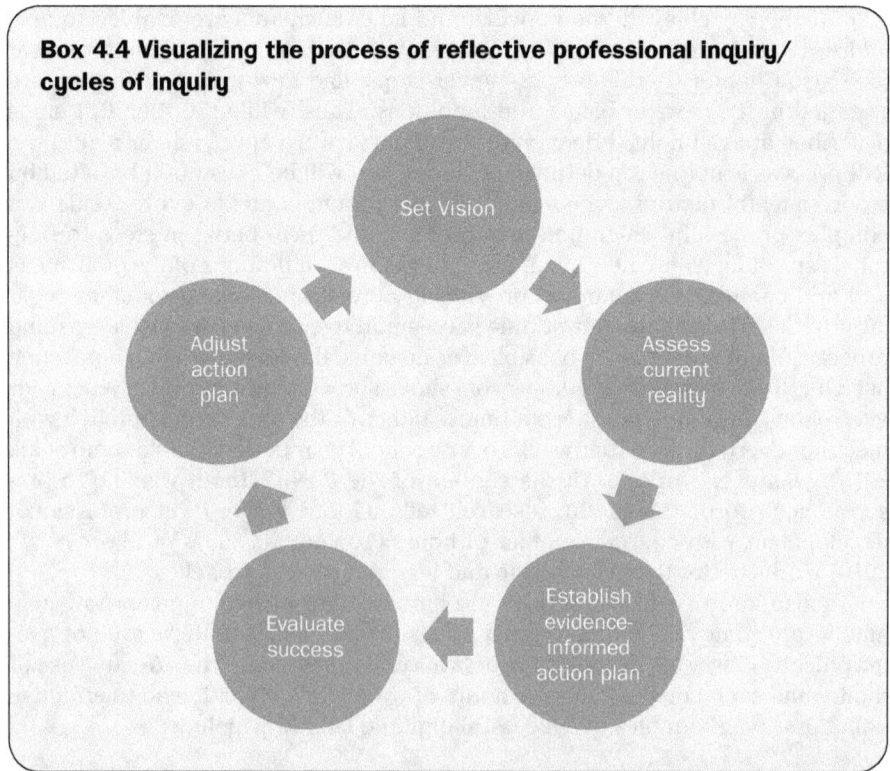

PLN outcomes in their educational practice (Brown and Flood, 2019). This process of creating, sharing and applying knowledge resulting from collaborative learning in PLNs (Poortman and Brown, 2021: 93) is called knowledge mobilization (KMb) (Finnigan et al., 2013; Rodway, 2015; Cooper et al., 2019; Malin and Brown, 2019) and is further discussed in Chapter 5. In Box 4.4, we show a generic approach to visualizing such a cycle of inquiry.

How do we know if RPI is occurring?

We would expect to see changes in teacher talk and action if we are successful in our approaches to RPI. But what should we be looking out for? In fact, there are a number of taxonomies that can be used to classify levels of RPI. For example, Sparks-Langer et al. (1990) provide a seven-level framework for assessing reflective discourse in relation to both problem identification and the development of potential solutions. These seven levels are presented in Figure 4.1.

Naturally, of course, how you collect such data is vital. As a practitioner, you may wish to simply look out for these instances. Alternatively, if you want to measure impact in a meaningful way, you may wish, for example, to use a questionnaire or evaluate the level of reflection in written work (such as lesson plans). Engaging with researchers can also be helpful here. Wherever possible, however, try and avoid using approaches such as self-report only, since these are likely to be subject to biases as respondents often try and tell you what they think you want to hear.

Figure 4.1 The seven-level framework for assessing reflective discourse (from Sparks-Langer et al., 1990)

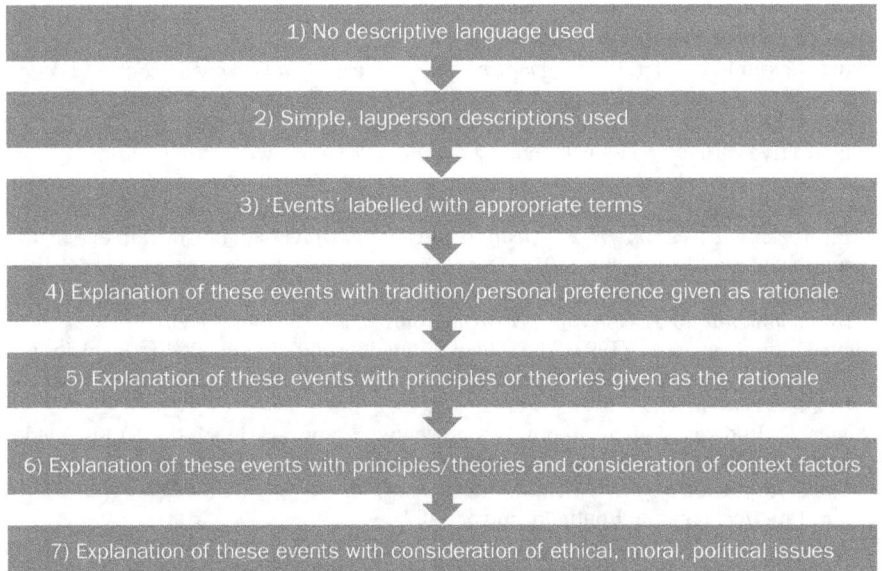

> **Chapter take-aways**
>
> - Reflective professional inquiry is a process in which teachers learn and innovate together and experiment in a goal-directed way, to improve their practice. RPI concerns participants' conversations in meetings, but extends beyond meetings to gathering literature and data, discussing colleagues' input, and continuing with ideas and feedback in the next meetings.
> - A key aspect of RPI involves evaluating both the process and outcomes of PLN-related interventions, for both teachers and students. As such, the RPI process is complex and iterative rather than simple and linear, and is centred on learning together how educational problems can be tackled and ambitions realized in an evidence-informed way.
> - What's more there are cultural considerations to take into account. For example, the historical norms regarding the innovation in question, as well as whether innovation generally, as well as inquiry-mindedness, is present within the school. Likewise, mobilization depends on trusting collaborative environments in which certain levels of risk-taking are acceptable.

References

Binkhorst, F. (2018) Balancing top-down and shared leadership: A case study of a teacher design team in transition to a new approach, in C. Brown and C.L. Poortman (eds) *Networks for Learning: Effective Collaboration for Teacher, School and System Improvement*. London: Routledge, pp. 20–37.

Brown, C. (2018) Research Learning Networks: A case study in using networks to increase knowledge mobilisation at scale, in C. Brown and C.L. Poortman (eds) *Networks for Learning: Effective Collaboration for Teacher, School and System Improvement*. London: Routledge, pp. 38–55.

Brown, C. and Flood, J. (2019) *Formalise, Prioritise and Mobilise: How School Leaders Secure the Benefits of Professional Learning Networks*. London: Emerald.

Brown, C., Poortman, C., Gray, H., Ophoff, J.G. and Wharf, M.M. (2021) Facilitating collaborative reflective inquiry amongst teachers: What do we currently know?, *International Journal of Educational Research*, 105: 101695.

Bryk, A., Sebring, P., Allensworth, E. and Luppescu, S. (2010) *Organizing Schools for Improvement: Lessons from Chicago*. Chicago, IL: University of Chicago Press.

Cheung, W.M. and Wong, W.Y. (2014) Does Lesson Study work? A systematic review on the effects of Lesson Study and learning study on teachers and students, *International Journal for Lesson and Learning Studies*, 3(2): 137–49.

Chinn, C. and Brewer, W. (1993) The role of anomalous data in knowledge acquisition: A theoretical framework and implications for science instruction, *Review of Educational Research*, 63(1): 1–49.

Cooper, A., Rodway, J., MacGregor, S., Shewchuk, S. and Searle, M. (2019) Knowledge brokering: 'Not a place for novices or new conscripts', in J. Malin and C. Brown (eds) *The Role of Knowledge Brokers in Education: Connecting the Dots Between Research and Practice*. London: Routledge, pp. 90–107.

Datnow, A., Park, V. and Lewis, B. (2013) Affordances and constraints in the context of teacher collaboration for the purpose of data use, *Journal of Educational Administration*, 51(3): 341–62.

Dick, S. and Peat, S. (2022) Scottish Island Schools Network: Bringing the remote rural voice to networked professional development, in G. Handscomb and C. Brown (eds) *The Power of Professional Learning Networks: Traversing the Present; Transforming the Future*. Woodbridge: John Catt, pp. 233–48.

Dudley, P. (2011) Lesson Study development in England: From school networks to national policy, *International Journal for Lesson and Learning Studies*, 1(1): 85–100.

Earl, L. and Timperley, H. (2008) Understanding how evidence and learning conversations work, in L. Earl and H. Timperley (eds) *Professional Learning Conversations: Challenges in Using Evidence for Improvement*. Berlin: Springer, pp. 1–12.

Finnigan, K. and Daly, A. (2012) Mind the gap: Organizational learning and improvement in an underperforming urban system, *American Journal of Education*, 119(1): 41–71.

Finnigan, K., Daly, A., Hylton, N. and Che, J. (2013) Systemwide reform in districts under pressure: The role of social networks in defining, acquiring, using, and diffusing research evidence, *Journal of Educational Administration*, 51(4): 476–97. Available at https://doi.org/10.1108/09578231311325668.

Greany, T. and Wolfe, A. (2022) Networking small rural schools in the pandemic, in G. Handscomb and C. Brown (eds) *The Power of Professional Learning Networks: Traversing the Present; Transforming the Future*. Woodbridge: John Catt, pp. 75–90.

Guskey, T. (2000) *Evaluating Professional Development*. Thousand Oaks, CA: Corwin Press.

Halbert, J., Kaser, L. and Koehn, D. (2011) Spirals of inquiry, building professional inquiry to foster student learning. Paper presented at ICSEI 2011, Limassol, Cyprus.

Kaser, L. and Halbert, J. (2017) *The Spiral Playbook: Leading with an Inquiring Mindset in School Systems and Schools*. Canada: C21 Canada.

Kools, M. and Stoll, L. (2016) *What Makes a School a Learning Organisation?*, OECD Education Working Papers, No. 137. Paris: OECD Publishing. Available at https://doi.org/10.1787/5jlwm62b3bvh-en.

Koutsouris, G. and Norwich, B. (2018) What exactly do RCT findings tell us in education research?, *British Educational Research Journal*, 44(6): 939–59.

Leithwood, K., Day, C., Sammons, P., Harris, A. and Hopkins, D. (2006) *Successful School Leadership: What it is and How it Influences Student Learning*, Research Report 800. London: DfES.

Lewis, C. (2000) Lesson Study: The core of Japanese professional development. Paper presented at the Annual Meeting of the American Educational Research Association, New Orleans, LA, 24–28 April.

Malin, J. and Brown, C. (2019) Joining worlds: Knowledge mobilization and evidence-informed practice, in J. Malin and C. Brown (eds) *The Role of Knowledge Brokers in Education: Connecting the Dots between Research and Practice*. London: Routledge, pp. 1–12.

Mitton, C., Adair, C., McKenzie, E., Patten, S. and Waye-Perry, B. (2007) Knowledge transfer and exchange: Review and synthesis of the literature, *Milbank Quarterly*, 85(4): 729–68.

Neal, J., Mills, K., McAlindon, K., Neal, Z. and Lawlor, J. (2019) Multiple audiences for encouraging research use: Uncovering a typology of educators, *Educational Administration Quarterly*, 55(1): 154–81.

Norman, D. (2013) *The Design of Everyday Things*. Cambridge, MA: MIT Press.

Poortman, C. and Brown, C. (2021) Guest editorial, *Journal of Professional Capital and Community*, 6(2): 93–8. Available at https://doi.org/10.1108/JPCC-04-2021-090.

Rodway, J. (2015) Connecting the dots: Understanding the flow of research knowledge within a research brokering network, *Education Policy Analysis Archives*, 23: 123. Available at https://doi.org/10.14507/epaa.v23.2180.

Rogers, E. (1995) *Diffusion of Innovations*, 4th edn. New York: Free Press.

Schildkamp, K. and Datnow, A. (2020) When data teams struggle: Learning from less successful data use efforts, *Leadership and Policy in Schools*, 21(2): 147–66.

Schildkamp, K. and Ehren, M. (2012) From 'intuition'- to 'data'-based decision making in Dutch secondary schools?, in K. Schildkamp, M. Lai and L. Earl (eds) *Data-Based Decision Making in Education: Challenges and Opportunities*. Dordrecht: Springer, pp. 49–67.

Schildkamp, K., Handelzalts, A., Poortman, C.L. et al. (2018) *The Data Team Procedure: A Systematic Approach to School Improvement*. Dordrecht: Springer International Publishing.

Schildkamp, K. and Poortman, C.L. (2022) Onderwijsverbetering door data-geïnformeerd werken [Improving education with data-informed decision making]. Available at https://www.onderwijskennis.nl/artikelen/onderwijsverbetering-door-data-geinformeerd-werken (accessed 21 October 2022).

Schildkamp, K., Poortman, C.L., Ebbeler, J. and Pieters, J.M. (2019) How school leaders can build effective data teams: Five building blocks for a new wave of data-informed decision making, *Journal of Educational Change*, 20(3): 283–325.

Schildkamp, K., Poortman, C.L. and Handelzalts, A. (2016) Data teams for school improvement, *School Effectiveness and School Improvement*, 27(2): 228–54.

Sebba, J., Tregenza, J. and Kent, P. (2012) *Powerful Professional Learning: A School Leader's Guide to Joint Practice Development*. Nottingham: National College for School Leadership.

Silins, H. and Mulford, B. (2004) Schools as learning organisations – effects on teacher leadership and student outcomes, *School Effectiveness and School Improvement*, 15(3–4): 443–66.

Sparks-Langer, G.M., Simmons, J.M., Pasch, M., Colton, A. and Starko, A. (1990) Reflective pedagogical thinking: How can we promote it and measure it?, *Journal of Teacher Education*, 41(5): 23–32.

Tschannen-Moran, M. (2004) *Trust Matters: Leadership for Successful Schools*. San Francisco, CA: Jossey-Bass.

Van Veen, K., Zwart, R.C., Meirink, J.A. and Verloop, N. (2010) *Professionele ontwikkeling van leraren: Een reviewstudie naar effectieve kenmerken van professionaliseringsinterventies van leraren*. ICLON/Expertisecentrum Leren van Docenten. Available at http://www.nro.nl/wp-content/uploads/2014/05/PROO+Professionele+ontwikkeling+van+leraren+Klaas+van+Veen+ea.pdf (accessed 4 November 2022).

Vangrieken, K., Meredith, C., Packer, T. and Kyndt, E. (2017) Teacher communities as a context for professional development: A systematic review, *Teaching and Teacher Education*, 61: 47–59.

Warren Little, J. (1990) The persistence of privacy: Autonomy and initiative in teachers' professional relations, *Teachers College Record*, 91(4): 509–35.

Wigman, K (2022) Towards an effective PLC: An intervention supporting reflective professional inquiry. Unpublished Master's thesis, University of Twente, Enschede.

Yoon, K.S., Duncan, T., Lee, S.W.Y., Scarloss, B. and Shapley, K.L. (2007) *Reviewing the Evidence on How Teacher Professional Development Affects Student Achievement*, Issues & Answers report, REL 2007–no. 033. Washington, DC: Regional Educational Laboratory Southwest. Available at https://ies.ed.gov/ncee/edlabs/regions/southwest/pdf/rel_2007033.pdf (accessed 4 November 2022).

Zala-Mezö, E. and Egli, J. (2022) What exactly happens during team meetings? Introduction of an analytical instrument and an overview of the results. Paper presented at the 2022 Virtual ICSEI conference.

5 The return – mobilizing findings and getting buy-in

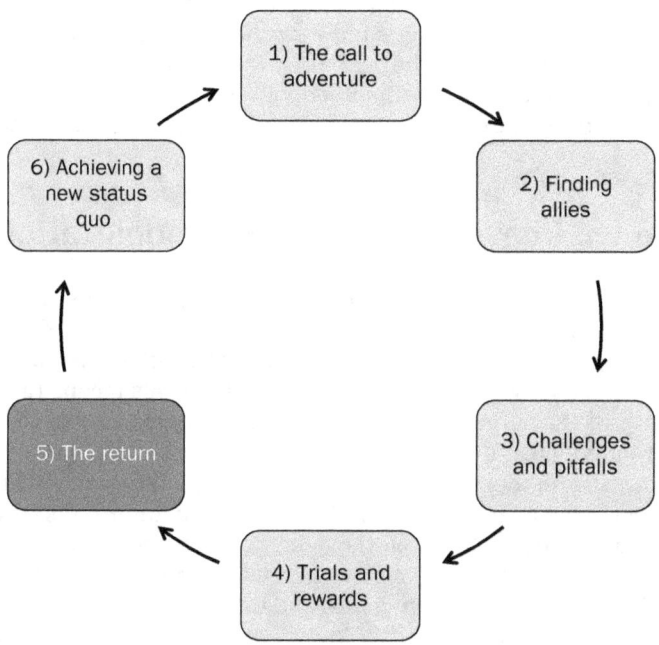

Mobilization is about making sure that PLN outcomes reach and are acted on in teachers' 'home schools'. It sounds simple, but the process of mobilization is actually quite complex, and all of us still have much to learn in this area. In this chapter, we will outline what is currently regarded as effective mobilization activity. In particular, we will show how mobilization is most impactful when school staff: i) actually engage with innovations; ii) collaboratively test out new practices that can be used to improve teaching and learning; and iii) continue to use and refine new practices in an ongoing way, so developing their expertise. Alongside this we also provide mobilization tools to help you establish and run such processes effectively, as well as signposting other areas to pay attention to, including school culture and thinking about who it is you are mobilizing to!

What is mobilization and why does it matter?

As we have seen, the learning and practice development that occurs in PLNs is likely to result in the development of an *innovation* – in other words, 'an idea, practice, or object that is perceived as new' by potential adopters (Rogers, 1995: xvii). The key to any innovation is the notion of *novelty* (Rogers, 1995). That is, if a potential user perceives some form of knowledge, practice, teaching program or product as new, it represents an innovation, regardless of any 'objective' novelty. The aim of a PLN, of course, is to engender the development and spread of effective practices across schools. Unfortunately, however, it is rare that innovations automatically spread from teacher to teacher like 'ripples in a pond' (Hubers, 2018). As a result, effort is required to encourage the engagement and take-up of new ideas, understanding or practices. This means that teachers and school leaders also need to understand how the innovation that emerges from networked learning activity can be best spread and harnessed, thus ensuring that other teachers and educators in their school engage with and adopt it – with teaching and learning (or other student outcomes) benefiting as a result.

What do we know about effective mobilization?

A key aspect of innovation mobilization is brokerage. The case for brokerage is nicely put by Hubers (2016: 73), who suggests schools are made up of multiple, overlapping groups. When individuals are not involved in a given group – for instance, if they are not participating in a PLN – this means that the work and practices of that group will be unfamiliar to them. As a result, it can be difficult for individuals to pick up on the group's work or outputs, because the meanings invested in them are often rooted in 'unspoken, tacit understandings that have developed over a long period of co-participation' (Hubers, 2016: 73). *Fractures* can then occur between the behaviours of those who participate in the group (and so have a shared history in relation to what it is doing, why and how to think about the problem in hand) and those who do not. These fractures are referred to as *boundaries*. Acts of knowledge brokerage that enable *boundary crossing* can help reduce these fractures or even prevent them occurring in the first place. Engaging in effective knowledge brokerage is, however, complex (Farley-Ripple et al., 2017). Essentially, this is because brokerage involves more than simply disseminating new knowledge, or informing individuals about new practices. Rather, brokerage is about effectively communicating innovation from one community to another such that it engenders changes in that community's understanding, *as well as* their actions.

With this in mind, a number of factors are likely to determine the extent to which knowledge brokerage occurs successfully. These include:

1 **The brokerage pathway:** i.e. do PLN participants seek to broker 'ready-baked' innovations, or will there be an element of innovation co-creation involved, such as through the use of within-school professional learning communities? Will everyone be brokered to, or just certain members of staff?

2 **The medium of brokerage:** for example, will brokerage occur face to face, through the use of a *boundary object*, or via a combination of these things? Furthermore, will participants be able to practise using the innovation in risk-free situations and environments?
3 **The characteristics of the broker:** e.g. who is brokering and what is their role and position *vis-à-vis* the organization and network of individuals they are brokering to?

We will now explore these three factors in more detail, using the case study of the Hampshire Research Learning Network as a learning tool. This means we can also introduce the notion of *distributed leadership* as one way of configuring the brokerage role. For more detail on distributed leadership, see Box 5.1.

> **Box 5.1 What is distributed leadership?**
> Over the last 20 years or so, the idea of distributed leadership has been increasingly prevalent in conversations about school leadership, worldwide. While there is no one universally accepted definition of the concept, distributed leadership is generally understood to involve an expanded understanding of school leadership beyond the activity of the school principal. At the same time, it is more than about just recognizing that there can be many leaders in a setting. Rather, distributed leadership represents a process through which decisions are actively made in relation to a greater pool of knowledge and experience, and with a greater ability to detect errors in decision-making, and because the people, practices and structures that make up the environment are involved in decision-making, the outcomes of decisions are more likely to be implemented (Boylan, 2018).
> The result is *empowerment*: distributed leadership leads to teacher self-efficacy and so creates schools that are both resilient and better placed to find innovative ways to tackle new challenges (Handscomb, 2011).
> The use of distributed leadership is also key to the effective mobilization of knowledge and innovation emerging from PLNs. This is because the interplay between network and school is an exemplar of what Kotter describes as *the dual system*. As Kotter (2014: 20) notes, 'in truly reliable, efficient, agile and fast enterprises, the network meshes with the more traditional structure ... it is not a super task force that reports to some levels in the hierarchy ... it is seamlessly connected and coordinated with the hierarchy ...'. In other words, Kotter's seamless meshing requires PLN participants to be afforded the autonomy and freedom associated with distributed leadership so that they can both innovate and successfully scale up the use of innovations.

The Hampshire Research Learning Network

Throughout the book we have touched on the idea of Research Learning Networks (RLNs): these are a specific type of PLN designed to enable the roll-out of new research-informed teaching practice at scale (Brown and Flood, 2019).

RLNs operate by establishing one (or more) PLNs with two to three participants from a number of schools, then using these participants to generate research-informed practices during a series of network workshops. Participants then work with their wider school colleagues to embed these practices in their 'home schools'. With this specific case we examine the *Hampshire Research Learning Network*, which operates across three schools in the South of England. We had previously been asked by PLN leaders to evaluate the working of the Hampshire RLN. To collect our evaluation data, interviews were held with 12 (out of 15) teachers involved in the network and survey data collected from 41 (out of 51) teachers, teaching assistants and school leaders from participants' 'home schools'.

Three dimensions of distributed leadership

Singaporian academics Hairon and Goh (2015) argue that we should seek out the existence of distributed leadership by examining the actual practices of individuals rather than their assigned roles or functions. Specifically, we should look for the presence of three dimensions of distributed leadership in the actions of school staff.

The first dimension is 'empowerment' – the ability or power of 'subordinates' to make decisions. Empowerment requires school leaders to relinquish power, albeit while still ensuring that the focus of distributed leadership is aligned and coheres with the priorities and values of the school (Hairon and Goh, 2015).

The second dimension of distributed leadership is 'interaction for shared decisions'. Here the notion of leadership corresponds to the influence that emerges as individuals at all levels engage with one another. When combined with the idea of empowerment, acts of influence can thus be initiated by anyone and flow in any direction. To necessitate this second dimension, we must ensure educators are able to interact effectively.

The third dimension is 'developing leadership'. This dimension suggests that distributed leadership can only function effectively when individuals in the organization have the required skills to engage in activities such as: 'rallying others towards common group goals, considering individual needs of group members in decision making, making decisions based on micro and macro contextual knowledge ... and promoting shared ownership and accountability' (Hairon and Goh, 2015). Key is that dimensions two and three cohere to ensure participative or shared decision-making amongst all members of staff.

Models of distributed leadership

Applying these three dimensions to the interview data, we (the second author of this book and a PhD student) found the existence of three models of distributed leadership used by Hampshire RLN participants to mobilize RLN innovations. In the first model (DL1), primarily evident in two of the RLN schools (St Swathes and Marchwood),[1] teachers participating in the RLN were empowered to make decisions regarding the RLN-related activity, with new ideas expected to permeate through being *championed* by advocates. For example, RLN participants were typically encouraged to influence colleagues by *persuading* them to adopt practices; the skills required to achieve this persuasion mostly corresponded to effective change management, for instance establishing a 'sense of urgency', or positioning adoption of innovations as a common goal to be achieved.

In the second model of distributed leadership (DL2), primarily evident in Northwood School, all teachers were empowered to make decisions regarding the development of new teaching and learning practices linked to the RLN, but the teachers participating in the RLN were empowered to facilitate this process as a collective endeavour. Here, influence occurred via collaborative inclusive decision-making, taking place in, for example, a within-school professional learning community (see Chapter 3). For example, as one senior leader noted about her school: 'we now have an in-school learning community that wasn't there before … where we use learning conversations as a basis for supporting and challenging each other'. The skills required for DL2 to flourish were identified as effective facilitation, as well as an awareness and understanding of the needs and aims of the organization. At Northwood, decision-making using DL2 was focused on a specific issue, was collective in nature and followed a relatively linear pathway, which moved from knowledge and discussion ⇨ decision-making ⇨ trialling and embedding. But DL2 could also occur as a process where individuals or small teams each have their own foci, situated within a common theme, and are supported to engage in a process of iterative exploration in relation to this focus. A variant of DL2, DL2+, thus occurred when the role of RLN participants was to facilitate an ongoing process of investigation within their school.

What else does our data show?

As we note in the introduction chapter, the purpose of PLNs is to build capacity; specifically, the capacity of all teachers connected to the PLN to learn, and for this learning to result in improved practice. Naturally such improvements in practice should then result in enhanced outcomes for children. Allied to this idea of capacity building is that of sustainability. Here capacity building should be viewed as something that is ongoing and that results in long-term changes in behaviour. At the same time, capacity and sustainability depend on teachers being more than just passive implementers of new practices; rather they need to be 'active change agents'. This means teachers should critically engage with, and refine, new practices to maximize their impact.

To ascertain which model of distributed leadership was most effective, therefore, we also sought to understand the extent to which teachers in participating

---

1 The names of all three schools have been changed to protect their anonymity.

schools not only learned about RLN-related innovations through interactions with their colleagues, but also whether they then engaged in a collaborative process of use, experimentation and refinement, in order to ensure these innovations delivered maximum impact. To try and verify this we first looked at the survey data on how teachers interact with one another (using a more formal version of the process we introduced in Box 2.5). This can be found in Figures 5.1 and 5.2. To help interpret the charts, it should be noted that:

- circles = teaching assistants
- squares = teachers
- triangles = middle leaders
- diamonds = senior leaders

Lines represent connections between teachers, teaching assistants, school leaders etc. (for example, a line might represent two teachers regularly conversing or collaborating).

To begin with, we examined whether there is simply conversation (i.e. basic levels of interaction) occurring around RLN-related outputs. Our findings are shown in the left-hand side of Figures 5.1 and 5.2. Here it can be seen that *just* conversation between staff in relation to RLN outputs seems to be much more prevalent in St Swathes and Marchwood, while less common in Cedric's and Northwood. Since conversation alone is insufficient for attaining *expertise*, which also requires the ongoing, hands-on use of an innovation, we also looked at how conversation is combined with other activity. Our findings can be found on the right-hand sides of Figures 5.1 and 5.2, which illustrate who survey respondents say they have conversations with *and* who they engage in collaborative professional development activities in order to trial and embed new approaches to teaching and learning. As we move away from conversation exchanges to explore relationships that require more interaction and collaboration,

Figure 5.1 Relationships between staff in St Swathes, Cedric's and Northwood Schools

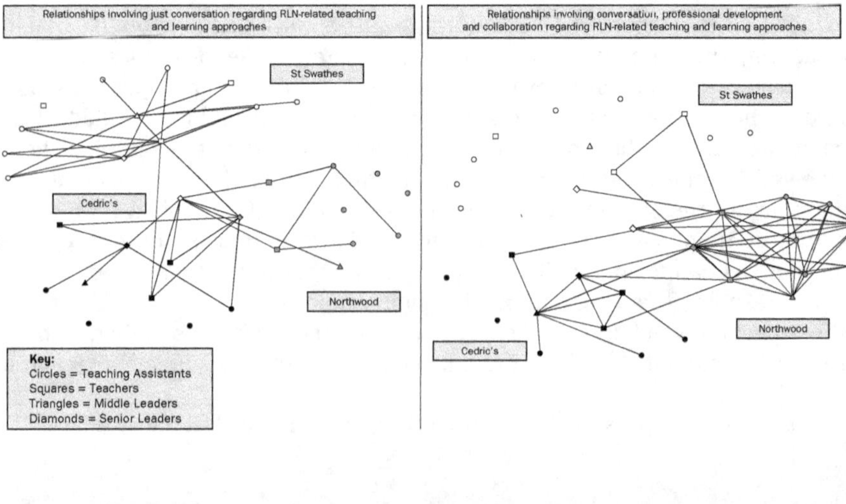

Figure 5.2 Relationships between staff in Marchwood School

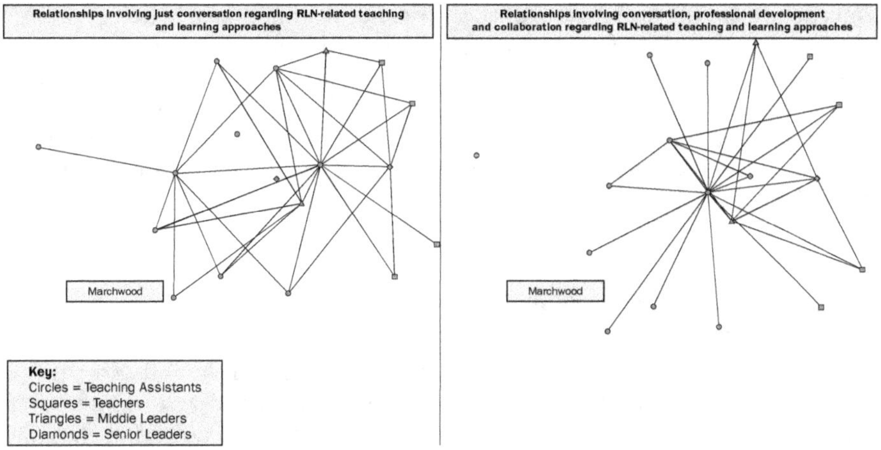

Relationships involving just conversation regarding RLN-related teaching and learning approaches

Relationships involving conversation, professional development and collaboration regarding RLN-related teaching and learning approaches

Key:
Circles = Teaching Assistants
Squares = Teachers
Triangles = Middle Leaders
Diamonds = Senior Leaders

we see that this is most prevalent in Northwood School and, to a lesser extent, in Cedric's School.

Use of RLN innovations

Our survey data also revealed *how* school staff were using RLN outputs. Survey respondents were asked to indicate the way in which they were using RLN-related innovations via a *Levels of Use* scale (Hall and Hord, 2001), a survey instrument designed to explore the take-up of innovation. Responses to the scale can be found in Table 5.1. As can be seen, the questions in the Levels of Use scale can be broadly divided into four 'use' types. These are: 'no use', which corresponds to respondents having little or no knowledge of new practices; 'preparing for use', where respondents are getting ready to begin using innovations, typically by finding out more about them and what their use entails; 'mechanical use', which is the use of new practices without reflection or any intention to change or improve the innovation. In other words, mechanical use involves employing an innovation in accordance with how one was shown or told to use it (and getting this use 'right'). 'Expert use', on the other hand, is when we begin to understand how our use of an innovation can be modified according to the specifics of a situation so that its impact can be improved. When it comes to teaching, expert use also involves the collaborative modification of new approaches to teaching and learning so that all students benefit.

Table 5.1 shows that in Cedric's School, just over half of respondents (55.5 per cent) suggested they were engaging in some form of expert use of the RLN-related innovations, with a fifth (22.2 per cent) engaging in some form of preparatory or mechanical use. For Northwood, *all* teachers were engaging either in expert (66.6 per cent) or mechanical use (33.3 per cent) of the RLN-related interventions. For Marchwood and St Swathes, however, usage was much more concentrated at the bottom end of the scale. For instance, nearly half of staff in Marchwood (45.5 per cent) were not using the innovations at all, with just over a third (36.4 per cent) preparing to use them or using innovations in a mechanical way. For St Swathes, 44.4 per cent of staff were either not using RLN-related innovations, or preparing for their use. A third of St Swathes' School staff were engaging in mechanical use, while just a fifth (22.2 per cent) were engaged in expert-level use.

So what does this mean?

From Figures 5.1 and 5.2 and Table 5.1 it can be seen that in both Northwood School and Cedric's, a more collaborative interactive approach ensured staff went beyond just the simple exchange of information, to engaging in behaviour that is likely to help them develop as expert users of these new practices. In turn, this behaviour serves to ensure that innovations are continually refined in order to maximize their impact for children and young people. Furthermore, our interview data also revealed three approaches to distributed leadership, directed at mobilizing outputs of the RLN. In the first of these models (St Swathes and Marchwood), RLN participants were responsible for developing new approaches to teaching and learning and then for encouraging their adoption by others. In the second model (Northwood), all teachers were empowered to make decisions in relation to new teaching and learning practices, but teachers participating in the RLN were responsible for facilitating this process. This particular approach to distributed leadership involved a learning conversation-type process within a professional learning community (see Chapter 3 for more on learning conversations). Specifically, the process involved all teaching staff being collectively focused on a specific issue, with RLN participants ensuring that teaching staff followed a series of steps that moved from an initial knowledge and discussion phase to a process of trialling and embedding. With the third approach to distributed leadership (Cedric's), RLN participants acted to facilitate a cycle of inquiry within their school. Here individuals and small teams each had their own foci, situated within a broader common theme, and were supported to engage in a process of iterative exploration in relation to this focus.

While each model is clearly different, each has the potential to facilitate capacity building as long as they enable types of collaboration that move beyond just the sharing of information and advice, to the active trialling of new teaching practice. At the same time, what we found above seems to indicate that models of distributed leadership that *actively* involve staff in decisions about what innovations to adopt and how to adopt them, are more successful in getting staff to:

1 **actually engage** with innovation;
2 really **test out how new practices can be used** to improve teaching and learning; and
3 **continue to use** and refine practices in an ongoing way.

Table 5.1 To what extent are school staff using the new approaches to teaching and learning relating to the RLN?

School*	Use type	C (n = 9)	N (n = 9)	M (n = 11)	S (n = 9)
I have little or no knowledge of these practices and no involvement with them.	No use	22.2%	0%	45.5%	11.1%
I am preparing for my first use of these practices.	Preparing for use	0%	0%	0%	22.2%
I have recently acquired or am acquiring information about these practices and/or have recently explored or am exploring their value and their demands for both myself and students.		11.1%	0%	18.2%	11.1%
I am focusing most effort on the short-term, day-to-day use of these practices with little time for reflection.	Mechanical use	11.1%	11.1%	9.1%	0%
I am now regularly using these practices and am confident in my ability to do so.		0%	22.2%	9.1%	33.3%
I am varying the use of the innovation to increase the impact on students within my immediate sphere of influence (e.g. my class or similar). Variations are based on knowledge of both short- and long-term consequences for students.	Expert use	11.1%	11.1%	0%	0%
I am combining my own efforts to use the practices with the related activities of colleagues to achieve a collective impact on students within our common sphere of influence (e.g. in a year group).		33.3%	44.4%	0%	11.1%
I am re-evaluating the use of the innovation, and am seeking major modifications or alternatives to achieve increased impact on students, and I am exploring new goals for myself and the school.		11.1%	11.1%	9.1%	11.1%
Other (please specify)		0%	0%	9.1%‡	0%

*C = Cedric's, N = Northwood, M = Marchwood, S = St Swathes. ‡'Refinement of the research focus'.

This doesn't necessarily mean that approaches to mobilization that use distributed leader 'champions' to promote the take-up of innovations are ineffective, but it is clear that if they are to work, then two things need to occur. First, such champions will only be successful when school leaders ensure that they can interact with others. Second, champions also need the capacity to lead. As well as promoting ideas, therefore, this involves activity such as illustrating the relative benefits of innovations and persuading others to adopt them (see Table 5.2). This means that distributed leaders undertaking this approach must have confidence, the presence, and understanding of (and ideally experience in) approaches to effective change management. If these things are lacking it seems unlikely that interaction alone will lead to the future adoption of an innovation. This requires school leaders to select their distributed leaders wisely, but also to support them in developing the skills they need to undertake their role effectively.

The type of knowledge involved in mobilization

Although there is a lot of insight to be had from the case study above, there are also some other useful points to consider when it comes to mobilizing innovation. To begin with we know that, all too frequently, potential adopters face uncertainty when deciding to adopt and use unfamiliar innovations. As a result, they often rely on perceived attributes of the innovation to make decisions. In particular, five attributes are thought to shape potential adopters' attitudes and decisions in relation to the innovation in question. These attributes concern an innovation's: relative advantage, compatibility, complexity, observability and trialability (Rogers, 1995; Neal et al., 2017). Detail on each of these is set out in Table 5.2, with adoption much more likely to occur when these characteristics are addressed.

At the same time, it is important to consider not only what knowledge is shared (i.e. what information could be provided that might influence thinking

Table 5.2 Five attributes affecting the adoption of innovations

Attribute	Conceptual definition (taken from Rogers, 1995: 15–16)
Relative advantage	The extent to which an innovation is perceived as better than the idea it supersedes
Compatibility	The degree to which an innovation is perceived as being consistent with the existing values, past experiences and needs of potential adopters
Complexity	The extent to which an innovation is perceived as difficult to use
Observability	How visible the results of an innovation are to others
Trialability	Whether and the extent to which an innovation may be experimented with on a limited basis

around these attributes), but also at what level it is shared. Here, information can be thought of as relating to one of four levels:

1 **Basic information:** what the members of the PLN are doing/have done.
2 **Underpinning knowledge:** the purpose underpinning what the members of the PLN are doing/have done (the *why* of what is being done).
3 **Underpinning practices:** information on how to do what members of the PLN are doing or what they have done (the *how* of what is being done).
4 **Combined knowledge and practice:** combining an explanation of the purpose underpinning what members of the PLN are doing/have done, with information on how to do it (the *why* and *how* of what is being done).

It is suggested (Rogers, 1995; Hubers, 2016; Brown and Graydon, 2017; Brown and Flood, 2018) that the last of these levels – a combination of information on both underpinning knowledge and underpinning practice – is key. A vital question, however, is what kind of detail will be required to enable this knowledge to not only be utilized, but also allow new practices to be customized and tailored to a given context. A possible answer to this is provided by the seven domains set out in Brown and Graydon's (2017) theory of action approach to mobilization:

1 The **context** in which the school or setting is situated.
2 The **problem or driver** for the **innovation**.
3 Detail on **the innovation** and how it was intended to result in change.
4 **Activities and interactions** related to the introduction and roll-out of the innovation.
5 The **learning** that results from teachers engaging in these activities/results from these interactions.
6 **Changes in teachers' behaviour**, and the extent to which an innovation is being used.
7 The **difference** behavioural changes have made to student outcomes.

What these seven domains provide is a way for educators in separate communities of practice or networks to understand the specific problem the innovation was designed to tackle (and the context in which that problem was situated), *why* it was believed the innovation would work, as well as *how* the innovation was actualized (e.g. in terms of the materials or protocols developed as part of the innovation, how educators were informed about the innovation, the people and resources educators had access to in order to support them in employing the innovation and so on). They also enable educators to assess whether using the innovation has been successful: for example, has the understanding of educators regarding the problem, and how it might be addressed, changed and how? What are educators now doing differently? And have changes in knowledge and behaviour led to desired changes to student outcomes? Answering the questions posed in Table 5.3 can help provide really

Table 5.3 Developing rich information on an innovation to support its mobilization

Theory of action domain	Questions to consider
1 Context	• What is the context of the school/group of schools in which you are situated?
2 Problem or driver for intervention	• What is the problem you were facing? • Who did it affect? • How long had it been going on for? • What were the underlying causes? Or, conversely, what was the motivation to innovate?
3 The intervention	• What did your intervention aim to do and how was it supposed to work? • Where does the intervention originate from and why? • Why did you think it would be effective (for instance, is it informed by research studies)? • Who was involved (who was intended to receive it and who rolled it out)?
4 Activities and interactions	• What were the activities involved in its roll-out (including detail on length, number of sessions, where activities will be held, etc.). • What encouragement, support or resources were offered or provided? • How were participating teachers made aware of the activities, support or resources? • How was it envisaged that participants would engage with these activities, support or resources? • Relevance – how was the intervention being introduced? • Reaction to the activity – how did participants respond? • How did participants' attitudes change?
5 Learning	• What learning resulted from the activities? • What new knowledge or skills did participants gain? • How did participants' understanding or perspectives change? • What access to new people was gained and how did this help with learning? • What access to new resources was gained (e.g. new tools, methods) and how did this help with learning? • Did participants have access to new sources of information? What new sources?
6 Changes in behaviour	• How was it intended that participants would use the intervention? • How were participants helped to feel confident to do what was required? • What support was provided to facilitate changes to participants' behaviour?
7 Difference	• What effect did the implementation have? • Were teachers more successful? How? • Were students more successful? How?

detailed information that enables other educators to adopt and successfully utilize your innovation (with information in relation to 5–7 potentially coming from approaches to measuring impact detailed in Chapter 4).

If attempts at brokerage can address these domains, they will not only show brokers why an innovation was developed, how it should be used and how success can be assessed – they simultaneously provide sufficient information to address perceptions regarding three of the characteristics posited by Rogers (1995) in Table 5.2. This is vital since such information will affect whether innovations are adopted or not. Specifically, providing the type of information set out in Table 5.3 means that educators can consider *compatibility* (can a new innovation easily fit alongside existing practices?), *complexity* (how difficult is the innovation to employ?), and *observability* (can impact be demonstrated?).

Who is being brokered to?

PLNs are designed to lead to the development and use of innovation at scale. If we examine Rogers' (1995) 'diffusion of innovations theory', however, it is clear that not everyone is likely to embrace innovation. Rogers (1995) classifies individuals' relationships with innovations according to whether they are: 1) innovators; 2) early adopters; 3) early majority; 4) late majority; or 5) laggards. The definitions of these adopter types are set out in Table 5.4.

It can therefore be seen that, according to Rogers, the vast majority of individuals adopt innovations only after someone else has already done so. This takes us back to the role of the change agent that was discussed in Chapter 2. Here, as you may recall, we suggested that change agents are those individuals best situated within a social network to mobilize the types of social capital needed to ensure a given change happens. More specifically, however, this means we need to select our change agents according to the level of social influence they have within a network. As we all know, social influence can have a material impact on people's attitudes and behaviours: in other words, our choices and decisions and our opinions and beliefs are, more often than not, influenced by others (Berger, 2016). But it is also clear that social influence can assert itself in a number of ways, including:

1. through implicit norms and guidelines that govern our understanding of how to respond in specific situations (Berger, 2016);
2. individuals can rely on the judgement of others when they are uncertain, meaning that the views of groups in such situations can converge (Asch, 1956);
3. individuals can also use the behaviour of others as a source of information to guide how to act – or as Berger observes, as 'a heuristic that simplifies decision making' (2016: 29) (Berger provides a myriad of examples to illustrate this point, ranging from where we park our car to how we decide which school to send our children to); and
4. that people often feel social pressure to conform with the decisions or behaviour of the wider group (Berger, 2016).

Table 5.4 Adopter types identified by Rogers (1995)

Adopter type	Definition (taken from Rogers, 1995: 264–5)	% of population
1 Innovators	When it comes to new ideas, innovators are active information-seekers. They have a high degree of mass media exposure and their interpersonal networks extend over a wide area, reaching outside of their organization. Furthermore, the innovator plays an important role – the launching of new ideas – by importing them from outside their organization's boundaries.	2.5
2 Early adopters	Early adopters are a more integrated part of the local system than are innovators, and have the greatest degree of opinion leadership. The early adopter is considered by many as 'the individual to check with' before using a new idea and serves as a role model for the rest of the organization.	13.5
3 Early majority	The early majority adopt new ideas just before the average member of the organization, but seldom hold positions of leadership. The early majority typically deliberate for some time before completely adopting a new idea.	34.0
4 Late majority	The late majority adopt new ideas just after the average member of the organization. Innovations are approached with a sceptical and cautious air, and the late majority do not adopt until most others have done so. Furthermore, almost all of the uncertainty about a new idea must be removed before the late majority feel it is safe to adopt.	34.0
5 Laggards	Laggards are the last of the organization to adopt an innovation. Typically the decisions of laggards are often made in terms of what has been done previously and laggards tend to be suspicious of innovation and change.	16.0

So, having on board a change agent who possesses social influence means you can seek to influence the take-up of new innovations using a myriad of approaches: from having the change agent explicitly promote the idea to actively using it, and being seen to actively use it. Of course, brokers will also need to be regarded by others as possessing expertise relevant to the subject matter of the PLN – a broker who is not seen as an expert in the area of innovation in question may struggle to engage others (Atteberry and Byrk, 2010).

> **Chapter take-aways**
>
> - Mobilization is about making sure that PLN outcomes reach and are acted on in teachers' 'home schools'. It is extremely rare that innovations automatically spread from PLNs to schools. As a result, effort is required to encourage the engagement and take-up of new ideas and practices. This means that teachers and school leaders need to be abreast of effective mobilization practice.
> - Our case study of the Hampshire RLN illustrated that effective mobilization leads to more than school staff simply knowing about an innovation; it also leads to them using the innovation in ways steeped in high levels of expertise. Here, collective and collaborative processes of knowledge-sharing, decision-making, and the trial and refinement of practices appear more impactful, seeming to result, ultimately, in staff using new practices in a more expert way.
> - Distributed leadership can be a great way to achieve effective knowledge mobilization. But at the same time, embracing distributed leadership also requires the school leader to recognize that their role must necessarily involve supporting distributed leaders to develop the skills they need to undertake their role effectively.

References

Asch, S. (1956) Studies of independence and conformity: A minority of one against a unanimous majority, *Psychological Monographs*, 70(9): 1–70.

Atteberry, A. and Byrk, A. (2010) Centrality, connection and commitment: The role of social networks in a school-based literacy initiative, in A. Daly (ed.) *Social Network Theory and Educational Change*. Cambridge, MA: Harvard Education Press, pp. 51–76.

Berger, J. (2016) *Invisible Influence: The Hidden Forces that Shape Behaviour*. New York: Simon & Schuster.

Boylan, M. (2018) Enabling adaptive system leadership: Teachers leading professional development, *Educational Management, Administration & Leadership*, 46(1): 86–106.

Brown, C. and Flood, J. (2018) Lost in translation? Can the use of theories of action be effective in helping teachers develop and scale up research-informed practices?, *Teaching and Teacher Education*, 72: 144–54.

Brown, C. and Flood, J. (2019) *Formalise, Prioritise and Mobilise: How School Leaders Secure the Benefits of Professional Learning Networks*. London: Emerald.

Brown, C. and Graydon, J. (2017) *An Evaluation of Renfrew County Catholic District School Board's Efforts to Deepen the Practice of Pedagogical Documentation Across Their District*. Renfrew, Ontario: Renfrew County Catholic District School Board.

Farley-Ripple, E., Tilley, K. and Tise, J. (2017) Brokerage and the research–practice gap: A theoretical and empirical examination. Paper presented at the 2017 annual meeting of the American Educational Research Association, San Antonio, Texas.

Hairon, S. and Goh, J. (2015) Pursuing the elusive construct of distributed leadership: Is this search over?, *Educational Management & Leadership*, 43(5): 693–718.

Hall, G. and Hord, S. (2001) *Implementing Change: Patterns, Principles and Potholes*. Boston, MA: Allyn & Bacon.

Handscomb, G. (2011) Fostering resilience through school leadership, in C. Day, A. Edwards, A. Griffiths and Q. Gu (eds) *Beyond Survival: Teachers and Resilience*. Nottingham: University of Nottingham, pp. 11–13. Available at https://www.nottingham.ac.uk/research/groups/crelm/documents/teachers-resilience/teachers-resilience.pdf (accessed 11 November 2020).

Hubers, M. (2016) *Capacity Building by Data Team Members to Sustain Schools' Data Use*. Enschede: University of Twente.

Hubers, M. (2018) *Q & A with Mireille D. Hubers*, Lead the Change Series, 82. Washington, DC: AERA Educational Change Special Interest Group.

Kotter, J. (2014) *Accelerate: Building Strategic Agility for a Faster-Moving World*. Boston, MA: Harvard Business School Press.

Neal, J., Neal, Z., Lawlor, J., Mills, K. and McAlindon, K. (2017) What makes research useful for public school educators?, *Administration and Policy in Mental Health and Mental Health Services Research*, 45(3): 432–46.

Rogers, E. (1995) *Diffusion of Innovations*, 4th edn. New York: Free Press.

6 Achieving a new status quo – making networks an everyday feature of school life

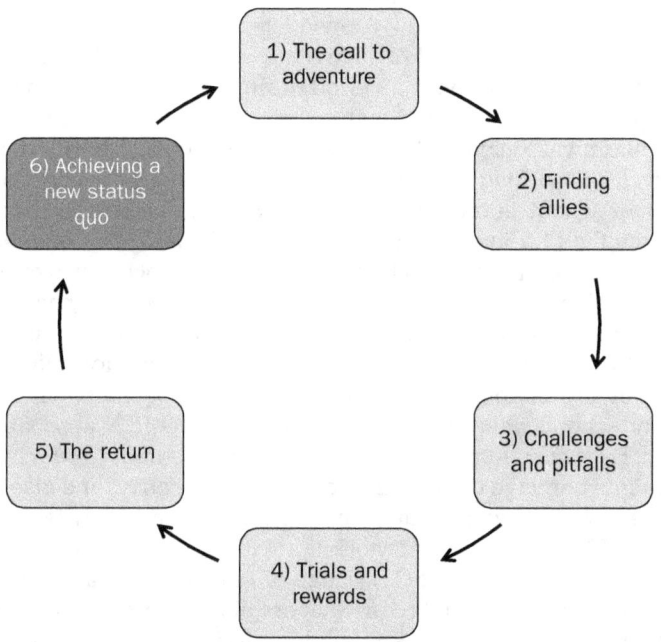

In this chapter, we conclude by exploring ways in which an evidence-informed PLN approach can be sustainably implemented in participating schools, both holistically and in an enduring, long-term way. Of course, in reality, this is not really *the* final step in the PLN process: the sustainability of school improvement in relation to any given PLN needs to be considered at the outset, or even before establishing a PLN, to ensure students can keep benefitting from the work in the long term. Following this, we then conclude with a PLN 'health check' to help readers with what they should now know and what they should attend to moving forward.

What is sustainability in the context of PLNs?

The sustainability of any educational innovation is all about integrating and scaling up core aspects of the innovation so that it becomes integral to schools' organizational routines, while also being malleable enough that it can adapt to ongoing work (Prenger et al., 2022; Tappel et al., 2022). The question is, however, whether i) the *PLN itself* is what continues long term; ii) whether we are just interested in continuing the outcome of PLN activity (such as, for instance, a new way of teaching, assessment, lesson materials); or iii) whether the *PLN way of working* is transported back and continued in the participating schools. (By PLN way of working we mean implementing collaborative, evidence-informed approaches in a scaled-up way in the participating schools, while not necessarily continuing the cross-school network.) Over the course of our work, we have seen different variants or combinations of i) to iii) in practice. Schools may decide to participate in networks for a fixed period of time and then only continue with the outcomes of the PLN work – for instance, new forms of teaching and/or assessment which were developed as a result of PLN activity. Schools may also participate in a cross-school PLN established for a period of time (ranging from one to multiple years) with external support, and may not continue after that external support has been withdrawn. Finally, schools may decide to continue with the evidence-informed way of working in one or more Professional Learning Communities (PLCs) in their school, in order to continue implementing outcomes for students resulting from the PLN and/or to address new problems. More often than not, it can be quite hard to continue with this way of working once any external support and facilitation have been withdrawn (which can also mean time to engage is withdrawn), even if individual PLN participants clearly see a benefit.

Many factors that have already been discussed in previous chapters relate to this issue of sustainability, and in this chapter we specifically focus on making sure that schools *as a whole* can benefit from the PLN approach over the longer term. Here current research suggests that the extent to which stakeholders/participants perceive the PLN approach to be effective, and also other individual characteristics, such as their motivation, or their knowledge about the goals of the PLN and its way of working, will all play an important role for sustainability (Prenger et al., 2022). Then, of course, there are various school organizational and contextual factors that are also important for sustainability. These are: i) collaboration, ii) knowledge mobilization, iii) school culture, iv) collegial support, v) staff turnover, and vi) leadership. Moreover, external support also has a role to play here. These factors have already been addressed in several places in previous chapters (e.g. collaboration in Chapter 3 and knowledge mobilization in Chapter 5). In the next sections, therefore, we will address each of these aspects for each of the phases of a PLN:

1 the start-up phase;
2 implementation; and
3 after external support has been withdrawn/when schools decide to continue with the PLN way of working in their own schools.

Please note that, in reality, these phases are not strictly distinct and the process is not linear.

Sustainability considerations in the PLN start-up phase

Achieving the sustainable implementation of any innovation is complex, and needs to be addressed even before schools start working with an innovation. This means that the innovation, on the one hand, and the school's vision, goals, individual teachers (motivation, and knowledge and skills), school organization and leadership, on the other, all need to be aligned and reflected in the working of the PLN and its process (Prenger et al., 2022; van den Boom-Muilenburg, 2022).

In previous chapters, we have already touched upon what is important from the start of PLN work, or even before. For example, starting and continuing fruitfully with a PLN would be hard without identifying and distinguishing between different types of problems of practice in order to develop a shared sense of purpose (ultimately focused on outcomes for students: see Chapter 1), or without, early on in the process, *finding allies* beyond school (e.g. in universities), in other schools and amongst our own teaching colleagues. Often, teaching and project timetables are established some six months in advance of the new school year, which means it will be quite hard to start up an initiative at the beginning of a new school year without this having been planned earlier. Fundamentally, therefore, this means that the intended PLN initiative needs to be aligned with school vision and policy as early as possible.

But school vision and school policies are also clearly fundamental to achieving sustainability. Vision is ideally developed with the input of all stakeholders, as well as effectively communicated and shared across the school (and beyond, e.g. with parents) (Tappel et al., 2022; van den Boom-Muilenburg, 2022). Policy is about the coherent formulation of goals, resources and materials, and time frames. This means that vision and goals, but also guidance and monitoring and evaluation need to be addressed. Only if vision and goals are formulated, discussed, adapted and aligned at an early stage will schools be able to decide how to monitor and evaluate progress in later stages. This does not only concern vision and goals related to the innovation, but also those related to the long-term vision on education in the school in general.

In terms of the PLN work itself, its characteristics *vis-à-vis* effectiveness and efficiency (as perceived by the stakeholders), a perceived systematic way of working, and the visibility of its progress are fundamental. If stakeholders do not see that working according to the PLN approach is effective, that it is worth the related time and budget, or that related steps and progress are clear, it will be hard to sustain. This also concerns parents and the larger (policy) context, such as the Education Inspectorate or the Ministry of Education, for example.

Leadership in relation to PLNs was discussed in detail in Chapter 3, but in Box 6.1 we augment this by referring to a tool that schools can use to reflect upon school leadership for sustainable innovation.

> **Box 6.1 School leadership reflection tool for sustainable innovation in schools**
>
> The following tool for reflection, derived from a study by Dutch academic Elske van den Boom-Muilenburg into the role of school leadership for sustainability,* provides a helpful way for school leaders to consider possible action required in relation to promoting PLN sustainability regarding the following (see: https://pro-u.reflectiontool.utwente.nl/en):
>
> 1. Organizing and (re)designing the organization;
> 2. Managing the teaching and learning programme;
> 3. Understanding and developing people; and
> 4. Organizational structures and social-cultural interactions.
>
> For example, in relation to the first category – Organizing and (re)designing the organization – school leaders are asked to reflect on vision and goals, with related questions including, for example: 'Has the innovation been discussed in the school and have the aims of the innovation been determined jointly?' Such questions are meant to bring about a discussion between school leaders and teachers, and help them plan and execute next steps to be able to make progress. Other colleagues also need to be involved in this process to be able to scale up the way of working in the school. As we note above, sustainable innovation is a process, which means that the tool can and should be used regularly (e.g. once or twice a year) to make sure schools are continuing as intended.
>
> ---
>
> * Research carried out by Elske van den Boom-Muilenburg (2021). The role of school leadership in schools that sustainably work on school improvement with professional learning communities, in a collaboration between ELAN Dept. of Teacher Development, University of Twente, and the University of Groningen. This study was made possible by the Netherlands Initiative for Education Research NRO (project number 405-17-811).

Sustainability considerations in the PLN implementation phase

Collaboration, knowledge mobilization and support during the PLN process and the ongoing implementation of the new innovation are school organization factors that all help support sustainability. Of these we have already discussed 'strong modes of collaboration' in Chapter 3, and knowledge mobilization in Chapter 5. Support, meanwhile, is about colleagues in the school giving each other feedback by sharing ideas, resources and/or materials, helping to further develop their insights, commitment and expertise. Making PLN work part of the daily school routine will either stand or fall depending on the commitment of individual stakeholders. Teachers feeling involved with their colleagues, students and the school as a whole, feeling motivated to develop their knowledge and skills, and to apply what they have learned from PLN participation, are all influencing factors here. It remains important to realize that throughout the process, even when the (original) PLN participants are satisfied about their PLN work and it has yielded important insights for improving outcomes for students, this does not automatically mean all other colleagues will be enthusiastic. They might still not even be aware of what the PLN work and outcomes entail, let alone be able to apply the insights gained in their daily teaching routine. We sometimes assume professional development outcomes in general, and PLN work outcomes in particular, spread in the school like ripples in a pond, but unfortunately (as we have so recently seen) this effective spreading only really happens with viruses! To engage the whole school in PLNs, so-called *key actors* (van den Boom-Muilenburg et al., 2022) – or change agents – need to broker different types of knowledge, making use of activities such as capacity building, knowledge management, and linkage and exchange activities. Examples of these are facilitating discussion or sending out newsletters about the PLN, and translating research outcomes into more practical formats.

Sustainability considerations after external support has been withdrawn

Often, PLNs and their concomitant innovations are considered only for the funded time period. Roles and tasks are divided, and the immediate concerns at hand (when will we start, with what problem and goal, who will participate?) are emphasized. Even if the question 'What are we expecting in relation to this project in five years?' is posed, it is unlikely that a well-considered answer will be formulated. Many schools we have worked with stress the importance of external support (and funding, which also helps free up time) to help them 'think out of the box' and make sure the core components of the work are maintained (along with the added impetus of external motivation – that there is some expectation by others that we deliver by a given point in time) (see also Box 6.2).

> **Box 6.2 Now what? How to continue after termination of external support**
>
> In the Dutch PLN project (also mentioned in Chapter 1), PLNs were co-funded by the Ministry and studied by the university for a maximum of four years. In the first years, there was room for developing a shared sense of purpose and a structured way of working. Most participants enjoyed participating and felt they were learning (a lot). Over the course of the project they applied their knowledge and skills by developing products such as lesson series and instruments for research in practice. Their PLN work was increasingly focused on student learning. Sustainability only became the subject of discussion in the second part of the project period (cf. Stoll et al., 2006). Participants reported that the role of school leadership in their schools generally needed a lot of improvement in relation to sustainability. Some school leaders considered teachers' PLN participation

as individual professional development only, for example, or were not even really aware of what the PLN was about. In some PLNs, however, both the facilitators and participants applied for more funding to continue.

Beyond the funded period, there was a large variety in how the PLNs (results) were implemented in participants' schools. There was some indication that the work was continued (on a larger scale) for the longer term in participants' schools. Examples are: starting new PLNs, facilitated by the same local universities; integrating the PLN (way of working) into research–practice partnership between participating schools and the local university facilitators; and participants starting PLNs based on the original PLN theme in their own school. Successful continuation varied, but in general the findings showed that school leadership is crucial for sustainable innovation, even before the work itself is started (see Box 6.1).

On the other hand, there are also schools that start positioning (teacher-) leaders to take over supervision, capacity building and knowledge mobilization before the external support is withdrawn. Sometimes, these leaders participate in professional development specifically focused on the facilitation role they will have to play once external facilitators have left. Schools and facilitators work out a model that works for their specific context, in time. In the Netherlands, an increasing number of 'knowledge utilization' products are being developed to help schools continue with educational innovation and/or help them apply what (researchers in) other schools have learned. The *Netherlands Initiative for Education Research*, for example, is bringing together practical research-informed knowledge and tools on a website platform (https://www.onderwijskennis.nl/) categorized by both sectors and educational themes. Likewise, the pan-European *Evidence Informed Practice for School Inclusion* project provides training, coaching tools and resources in order to promote self-sustaining Research Learning Networks that can continue to generate and disseminate knowledge on inclusive educational practices once external funding has finished (see https://eipsi-project.eu for more). Universities are increasingly publishing 'open access', as well as producing tools that schools can use (independently) in practice. Often, the studies on which this practical knowledge and tools are based, result from intensive collaboration between researchers and practitioners (and researcher-practitioners). Together, we can achieve a lot in making PLN work sustainable for improvement in outcomes for students.

To help you think about the 'health' of your PLN work in different phases, Box 6.3 contains a PLN 'health check' that we recommend consulting (at least) in the start-up phase, during the PLN process and towards the planned final phase (before external support/funding is withdrawn). The chapters of this book provide more detailed information, examples and tools that you might want to return to with each main step. Although Chapters 1 and 2 might seem more relevant in the first phases and Chapters 5 and 6 more at the end, please keep in mind that this is not about a simple linear process, and aspects of different chapters can be relevant in different phases and recurrently.

Box 6.3 PLN health check

The statements below are related to the chapter take-aways. They can be used to monitor progress regularly (and at least in the start-up, during and final phases) in different ways. For example, you could plan to reflect on the entire checklist every two to three months with all PLN members, focusing on particular elements in different meetings; you could first reflect individually and then discuss in smaller teams before you have a plenary discussion, and/or you could decide to use the checklist particularly when you feel that progress is slow or when you experience resistance in the PLN and/or the related schools. There is no single way to make use of this health check, but we would like to emphasize one final time that all of its elements are interrelated, that the PLN process is iterative and complex, and sometimes it might feel like 'two steps forward, one step back'. At the same time, if you and your colleagues manage to keep in mind these steps as you go along, you will avoid many of the common challenges and pitfalls, so enhancing the chances of your PLN leading to improved student outcomes in the long term. And perhaps then a new *call to adventure* will start!

Reflect on these statements using 'no/on our way/yes'-type responses, and include specific examples to illustrate your answers. Please note it is not about a 'score', but about determining next steps in case they need to be taken. Make sure, therefore, that (collaborative) reflection is always followed by a concrete plan of action.

1 **Realizing the need for change:**
   a Our PLN starts with a problem that we are unable to tackle alone.
   b PLN participants agree on one or more goals focused on concrete outcomes for students.
   c We have used data and experiences about the current situation to help formulate the problem.
   d We have formulated one or more concrete goals showing what will specifically change for the better in terms of outcomes for students.

2 **Finding allies:**
   a We have found allies (i.e. a university) with whom to form a partnership that can support a structured way of working and reflective engagement centred on academic research and data.
   b We have found allies in other schools facing similar circumstances (i.e. similar levels of attainment, operating in similar contexts, that have shared histories) but without a risk of competition for students impeding our collaboration.

c Within the school, we have identified teachers who we need to work with to ensure change happens. The criteria that we have used for this are: school leader support; buy-in to the change leadership role by colleagues; access to training and professional development; and the change agent having a sense of self-efficacy with regard to their role.

3 **Challenges and pitfalls:**

a Our PLN participants and the colleagues in our schools are engaged in actively trying to innovate our practices related to the PLN goal in an ongoing way.
b We are aware of and actively working on optimizing the conditions that need to be in place for PLNs to endure and be successful:

   i a shared sense of purpose, centred on student learning;
   ii a spirit of trust and mutual dependence;
   iii a commitment to reflective inquiry;
   iv effective leadership;
   v joint work (for meaningful enquiry).

c We have arranged support by a facilitator who has the skills to convene PLNs, catalyse PLN activity, and to coach both participants and relevant school leaders.

4 **Adopting cycles of inquiry:**

a Our PLN is engaging in cycles of inquiry to learn and innovate together to improve our practice. Activities include gathering literature and data, discussing colleagues' input, and continuing with ideas and feedback in subsequent (PLN) meetings.
b We are evaluating our process and outcomes both at the student and teacher level and are aware of our PLN-related learning process as educators in relation to our PLN goal focused on outcomes for students.
c We are taking into account cultural considerations in the inquiry process, e.g. regarding inquiry-mindedness in our schools, and trust in relation to knowledge mobilization.

5 **Mobilizing findings and getting buy-in:**

a We know that our PLN-related knowledge and innovation do not automatically spread to others in our schools, and we are working actively on knowledge mobilization.
b We are ensuring knowledge mobilization moves beyond colleagues merely 'knowing about' our PLN work. For instance, we are using collective and collaborative processes of knowledge-sharing, decision-making and the trial and refinement of practices.
c The school leaders involved in our PLN recognize that their role involves supporting distributed leaders to develop the skills they need to undertake their knowledge mobilization role effectively.

6 **Making networks an everyday feature of school life:**

   a We considered the sustainability of our PLN, even before it began, and are regularly reviewing our progress in this respect, to make sure colleagues and students can benefit also in the long term.

   b We have determined (and are reviewing during the process) that sustainability for us represents [please choose as many relevant options as required]:

   i   the *PLN itself* continuing long-term;
   ii continuing the *outcome* of PLN activity (such as, for instance, a new way of teaching, assessment, lesson materials);
   iii the PLN *way of working* being transported back and continued in participating schools (i.e. it involves implementing collaborative, evidence-informed approaches in a scaled-up way in the participating schools).

   c We are taking into account the health check indicators from previous chapters that impact sustainability, and also focus specifically on:

   i   in the start-up phase:

   - school vision and policy alignment with the PLN;
   - PLN work characteristics *vis-à-vis* effectiveness and efficiency (as perceived by the stakeholders); a perceived systematic way of working, the visibility of its progress, and school leadership;

   ii in the implementation phase of the PLN: collegial support (i.e. collaboration and knowledge mobilization, supported by key actors);
   iii for the phase after external support has been withdrawn:

   - positioning (teacher-)leaders to take over supervision, capacity building and knowledge mobilization;
   - making use of practical tools developed during the supported phase to enable us to continue with the innovation and/or apply what has been learned; as well as using (professional) open-access publications, resulting from intensive collaboration between researchers, practitioners and/or researcher-practitioners.

References

Prenger, R., Tappel, A.P.M., Poortman, C.L. and Schildkamp, K. (2022) How can educational innovations become sustainable? A review of the empirical literature, *Frontiers in Education*, 7: 970715. Available at https://doi.org/10.3389/feduc.2022.970715.

Stoll, L., Bolam, R., McMahon, A., Wallace, M. and Thomas, S. (2006) Professional learning communities: A review of the literature, *Journal of Educational Change*, 7(4): 221–58.

Tappel, A.P.M., Poortman, C.L., Schildkamp, K. et al. (2022) Distinguishing aspects of sustainability, *Journal of Educational Change*. Available at https://doi.org/10.1007/s10833-022-09465-3.

Van den Boom-Muilenburg, S.N. (2022) *The Role of School Leadership in Schools that Work Sustainably on School Improvement with Professional Learning Communities*. Enschede: University of Twente.

Van den Boom-Muilenburg, S.N., Poortman, C.L., Daly, A.J. et al. (2022) Key actors leading knowledge brokerage for sustainable school improvement with PLCs: Who brokers what?, *Teaching and Teacher Education*, 110: 103577.

Index

Page numbers in italics are figures; with 'n' are notes; with 't' are tables.

Actualized Leadership Profile tool 25
agency 24
aid and assistance (collaboration) 35
allies 16–17, 85–6
   co-opting teachers in the home school 24–6
   other schools 19–20
   outside expertise and knowledge 17–19
   teaching colleagues 20–4

Balanced Leadership Profile® tool 25
baseline 6, 7–8
Begley, P. 5
Berger, J. 75
bottom-up change agents 24
brokerage 64–5, 75–7, 76t
Brown, C. 10, 25, 27, 73

Campbell, Joseph, *The Hero with a Thousand Faces* vii
capacity building 9, 43, 67
challenges and pitfalls 33–4, 86
   collaboration 34–7
   leadership 40–3
   reflective professional inquiry 37–9
   running the PLN 43–4
   shared sense of purpose 34
   trust 37
change, drivers for 3–5
change agents 20–8, 67, 75, 77, 83
Cheung, D. 25–6
Church of England Foundation for Educational Leadership 58
cognitive dissonance 11, 49
collaboration 2, *2*, 34–7, 80
conversation
   learning 38–9
   reflective 49–52
cultural competence 24
cultural norms 55, 56
cycles of inquiry 48, 57–9, 86

data capture mats 6, 9, 11, *13*
data collection, baseline 8
data teams 17–18, 51
Datnow, A. 22, 57
Day, C. 4–5
diffusion of innovations theory 75
distributed leadership 26, 27–8, 65, 66–9, *69*, 70
Dutch Ministry of Education 5
Dutch national PLN project 19, 83–4

early adopters 75, 76t
early majority 75, 76t
emotion, and RPI 56–7
empowerment 65, 66
Evidence Informed Practice for School Inclusion project 84
exchange and coordination 2, *2*
expressive social capital 21
external support 87
   and sustainability 80, 83–5

Flood, J. 27
Flórez, M.T 12–13
Fraser, P. 2
Fulop, G. 2

Germany, homogenous networks 19–20
goals 3, 5, 81, 82, 85, 86
   and the reflective professional inquiry process 52-3
   and shared sense of purpose 34, 42
Goh, J. 66
governance of the PLN 43–4
Graydon, J. 73

Hairon, S. 66
Hampshire RLN 65–6, 66–70, *68–9*, 77
Hattie, J. 10, 12–13
health check (PLN) 85–7
homogeneous networks 19
homophily 23
Hubers, M. 64

Index

implementation phase 80, 82–3, 87
influence, social 75, 77
innovations 64, 69–70, 71t, 72–5, 72t, 73, 74t, 76t
innovators 75, 76t
inquiry cycles 48, 57–9, 63–5, 86
instrumental social capital 21
interaction for shared decisions 66

Japan, Lesson Study 36
Johansson, O. 5
Joint Practice Development (JPD) 36, 55
joint work (collaboration) 35

key actors *see* change agents
knowledge creation 9, 38–9
knowledge mobilization (KMb) 59, 63–5, 72–5, 72t, 74t, 80, 86
knowledge utilization products 84
Kotter, J. 65

laggards 75, 76t
Lai, E. 25–6
late majority 75, 76t
Lazarsfeld, Paul 23
leadership 40–3, 82
   developing 66
   distributed 26, 27–8, 65, 66–9, *69*
learning 16–17
learning conversations 38–9
learning organizations (LOs) 55
Lesson Study 36, 51
literature review 9–10

Merton, Robert 23
mobilization, knowledge (KMb) 59, 63–5, 72–5, 72t, 74t, 80, 86

Nonaka, I. 38n
Norman, Donald 56
novelty 64

online PLNs 35–6, 58
opinion-formers 17, 25, 27
organizational semiotics 22

policy, school 81
process, RPI 52–4
professional development 27, 83, 84
Professional Learning Communities (PLCs) 80

professional learning networks (PLNs) (defined) vi–viii, *vii*

reflective professional inquiry (RPI) 37–9, 48
   assessing 59, *59*
   cycles of inquiry 57–9
   and emotion 56–7
   process 52–4
   and school environment 55–6
relationship builders 24
research, educational 18
Research Learning Networks (RLNs) 5–6, *7*, 9, 17, 27
   and data teams 17–18
   Hampshire RLN 65–6, 66–9, *68–9*, 77
   and reflective conversations 50–2
research methodology, baseline data 8
research strips exercise 10, 11, *12–13*
the return 63
   Hampshire RLN 65–6, 66–70, *68–9*, 71t, 77
   mobilization 72–5, 72t, 74t
Rogers, E. 75

Sammons, P. 4–5, 12–13
Schildkamp, K. 22, 51, 57
Scottish Islands School Network 58
self-improving school systems 20–1
seven-level framework 59, *59*
sharing (collaboration) 35
social capital 21–2, 34, 75
social influence 75, 77
social network analysis 25
social network theory 25
social networks 21–4, 55
Sparks-Langer, G.M. 59
start-up phase 3, 81–2, 87
Stoll, L. 10
storytelling and scanning (collaboration) 35
support, external 80, 83–5, 87
sustainability 79–81, 87
   after withdrawal of external support 80–1, 83–5
   implementation phase 80, 82–3
   and the start-up phase 80, 81–2
sustainable school improvement 57

Teacher Change Agent Scale 25
Teacher Engagement Networks (TENs) (New South Wales) 3

Teacher Learning and Leadership
    Program (TLLP) (Ontario) 3–4
technology 57–8
    online PLNs 35–6, 58
theory of action approach 73, 74t
top-down change 24–6
trust 37, 39
    and the school environment 55–6

Van den Boom-Muilenburg, S.N. 82
vision, school 81

Warren Little, J. 35, 55
*What Makes a School a Learning
    Organisation?* (OECD) 55
Wiliam, D. 12–13
workshops, RLN 6, 50, 57

www.ingramcontent.com/pod-product-compliance
Lightning Source LLC
Chambersburg PA
CBHW051119230426
43667CB00014B/2648